Twayne's English Authors Series

EDITOR OF THIS VOLUME

Kinley E. Roby

Northeastern University

Virginia Woolf

TEAS 243

drawing by Leonard Trawick

Virginia Woolf

VIRGINIA WOOLF

By SUSAN RUBINOW GORSKY

Cleveland State University

GEORGE PRIOR PUBLISHERS
London, England

TWAYNE PUBLISHERS
A Division of G. K. Hall & Co.
Boston, Massachusetts, U.S.A.

Copyright © 1978 by G. K. Hall & Co.

Published in 1978 by Twayne Publishers,
A Division of G. K. Hall & Co.
All Rights Reserved

Printed on permanent/durable acid-free paper and bound
in the United States of America

First Printing

This edition is published in the United Kingdom by George Prior
Associated Publishers Ltd., 37 - 41 Bedford Row,
London, W.C.1, England.

ISBN 0-86043-305-6

Library of Congress Cataloging in Publication Data

Gorsky, Susan R
Virginia Woolf.

(Twayne's English authors series ; TEAS 243)
Bibliography: p. 163 - 68
Includes index.
1. Woolf, Virginia Stephen, 1882 - 1941
Criticism and interpretation.
PR6045.072Z654   823'.9'12   78-8045
ISBN 0-8057-6712-6

To Buzz

Contents

About the Author

Susan Gorsky is an Associate Professor of English at Cleveland State University. She has been on the faculty there since 1969, when she received her Ph.D. in English literature and language from Case Western Reserve University.

She has published articles in *Modern Fiction Studies, Modern Drama,* and *The Journal of Popular Culture,* as well as anthologies and other journals. Her major research interests are experimental form in modern literature (including the dance-plays of William Butler Yeats and the novels of Virginia Woolf) and nineteenth-century fiction, especially that written by or about women. She is currently writing a book on the relationship between literary convention and social reality in the portrayal of men and women in late nineteenth and early twentieth-century British fiction.

Preface

In her novels and stories, in her essays of literary and social criticism, and in her life, Virginia Woolf speaks for the modern period. Modernism is the most important aesthetic movement of the twentieth century. Along with such experimenters as Joyce, Eliot, Yeats, Faulkner, and Lawrence, Virginia Woolf is a prime representative of those so strongly affected by the tumultuous transition to the current century. The activity of the many Woolf scholars suggests both her importance and the complexity of her works. Her novels and essays are not inaccessible; in fact they are largely free of the surface obscurities which characterize the work of some of her contemporaries. Although it is brightened by a genuine love of life, her vision is very nearly one of despair. Her novels represent a valiant attempt to assert order, but that order finally succumbs to the underlying sense of reality as chaos. Her experimentation led her to write novels whose intricacy, subtlety, and delicacy may frustrate or alienate the uninitiated reader. But these same qualities, properly identified, can become a source of fascination. It is the purpose of this study to be a unified introduction to Virginia Woolf as literary and social theoretician, fiction writer, human being, and representative of the modernists.

Virginia Woolf's critical essays cogently explain her aesthetic theories and at the same time offer insight into the quest for form and meaning characteristic of early twentieth - century art. Her social criticism is most frequently about the roles of women (especially women artists) in a period of intense change. Her short fiction, often strange and impressionistic, represents some of her earliest attempts to redefine in literary form the prevailing new ideas about people and their world which helped to change literature into what we recognize as "modern." In her life too, Virginia Woolf expresses the concerns of her time, from the function and possibilities of the artist and the role of women to the effect of two world wars. The experimental nature of her novels is in accord with the best of the modern era, and their sensitivity aligns them with the best of all time.

Because this book is an introductory guide, it has seemed appropriate to touch on as many aspects of Virginia Woolf's achievement as possible. Thus there are sections on her life and times, her aesthetic theories, her feminism, and so on, but most of the book is about her fiction. It is as a novelist that Virginia Woolf is best known; it is her novels which have been most closely scrutinized under scholarly microscopes. And it is the novels which deserve—and will receive—the greatest attention here. It has seemed appropriate to approach the novels in as many ways as possible: the author's intentions and accomplishments, the novels' themes, structure, style, language, plot, imagery, characterization. No single book could cover such a list in adequate depth. Each novel cannot be analyzed for all its component parts and each item on the list cannot be dealt with fully. Whole books and many articles have been written about the individual novels, about Virginia Woolf's use of symbolism, point of view, or sentence structure. For the interested reader, the annotated bibliography lists important books and explains where to find additional books and articles. In this study, the reader will find discussions of the *major* themes and stylistic components, and the interrelationship between form and meaning in Virginia Woolf's novels, and can hope to gain an overview of the life and art of this very important modern writer.

Acknowledgments

My thanks for their encouragement and advice go to my colleagues at Cleveland State University, especially to Professors Louis T. Milic and Elizabeth MacAndrew, and to the typists of the University's Word Processing Center. Special appreciation goes to Professor Leonard M. Trawick who, in the best Bloomsbury tradition, created an original drawing for the frontispiece of this book. My greatest thanks, for the greatest patience and interest, go to my husband, to whom this book is dedicated.

For *Jacob's Room and The Waves, To the Lighthouse*, and *Between the Acts*, all by Virginia Woolf, and for *Collected Essays, Volume 2*, edited by Leonard Woolf: for distribution in the United States, its dependencies, and the Philippine Islands, excerpts from the works of Virginia Woolf are reprinted by permission of Harcourt Brace Jovanovich, Inc.; copyright, 1920, by George H. Doran and Company; copyright, 1928, by Virginia Woolf; copyright 1922, 1927, 1929, 1931, 1933, 1941, by Harcourt Brace Jovanovich, Inc.; copyright, 1948, 1950, 1953, 1954, 1955, 1956, 1957, 1959, 1961, 1966, 1967, 1969 by Leonard Woolf. Permission is also granted by Harcourt Brace Jovanovich for reprinting excerpts from the following works: *Night and Day, Orlando, The Voyage Out, A Room of One's Own, Flush, Contemporary Writer, Roger Fry, Mrs. Dalloway, The Years, Three Guineas,* "Lappin and Lapinova" from *A Haunted House,* all by Virginia Woolf; *Collected Essays Volumes 1, 3,* and *4,* and *A Writer's Diary,* edited by Leonard Woolf; *Virginia Woolf and Lytton Strachey: Letters,* edited by Leonard Woolf and James Strachey; *Beginning Again* and *Downhill All the Way,* by Leonard Woolf; and *Virginia Woolf: A Biography.* by Quentin Bell.

For distribution throughout the world, less the U.S.A., its dependencies, and the Philippine Islands: permission to include extracts from Virginia Woolf's work is granted by the Author's Literary Estate and the Hogarth Press; permission to include the extracts from Leonard Woolf's work is granted by the Author's Literary Estate and the Hogarth Press; and permission to include the extracts from Quentin Bell's Biography is granted by the author and by Hogarth Press.

Chronology

1882   (Adeline) Virginia Stephen born in London on January 25, the third of four children of Leslie and Julia Duckworth Stephen.

1895   Death of Julia Stephen; Virginia's first suicide attempt.

1897   Marriage and death of Stella Duckworth Hills.

1902   Leslie Stephen knighted.

1904   Death of Leslie Stephen; Vanessa, Thoby, Virginia, and Adrian Stephen move to 46 Gordon Square, Bloomsbury. Virginia's first publication, an unsigned review (in *The Guardian*).

1906   Thoby Stephen dies of typhoid.

1907   Vanessa Stephen marries Clive Bell; Virginia and Adrian move to 29 Fitzroy Square.

1910   First Post Impressionist Exhibition.

1911   Virginia and Adrian share a house with John Maynard Keynes, Duncan Grant, and Leonard Woolf.

1912   Virginia marries Leonard Woolf, August 10.

1913   Virginia's first novel, *The Voyage Out* (earlier called *Melymbrosia*), completed after more than five years; accepted for publication by her half-brother, Gerald Duckworth. Publication delayed because of Virginia's breakdown. Suicide attempt.

1914   War declared, August 4.

1915   Virginia starts keeping a diary. *The Voyage Out* published.

1917   Virginia contributing regularly to *Times Literary Supplement*. Woolfs begin operating Hogarth Press in their Richmond home; first publication includes Virginia's short story, "The Mark on the Wall."

1918   Armistice Day, November 11.

1919   *Night and Day*, the second novel, published by Duckworth. Hogarth publishes two collections of her stories, *The Mark on the Wall* and *Kew Gardens*.

1921   More short fiction, *Monday or Tuesday*, published.

1922   *Jacob's Room*, the third novel, published by Hogarth Press which from this time handled all her British publications. Also accepted by Harcourt, Brace, after this her American publisher.

1925   Fourth novel, *Mrs. Dalloway*.
          The Common Reader, essays.

1927   Fifth novel, *To The Lighthouse*.

1928   Virginia travels with Vita Sackville-West for a week. *Orlando*, the first fictional biography.

1929   *A Room of One's Own*.

1931   Sixth novel, *The Waves*.

1932   Death of Lytton Strachey.
          The Common Reader: Second Series, essays.

1933   The second fictional biography, *Flush*.

1934   Death of Roger Fry.

1935   *Freshwater, A Comedy in Three Acts*, Virginia Woolf's only play, performed for friends.

1936   King Edward abdicates.

1937   Seventh novel, *The Years*, published after delays caused by illness.

1938   *Three Guineas*.

1939   War declared, September 3.

1940   *Roger Fry: A Biography*.
          Draft of eighth novel, *Between The Acts*, completed.

1941   Virginia Woolf dies, March 28, by drowning in the River Ouse.

1969   Death of Leonard Woolf.

CHAPTER 1

The Life of an Artist

I *Backgrounds: the Beginnings of Modernism*

ON January 25, 1882, a daughter was born to Leslie and Julia Stephen: Adeline Virginia, who was to become one of England's foremost writers and to be widely known under her married name, Virginia Woolf. At this time, Victorian England was becoming increasingly aware of the tumultuous change which introduced what today is called the modern age. This period of upheaval witnessed frequently disruptive events in history and literature. The breakdown of the traditional Western family and of class structure, the coming of a major economic depression, the accelerated shift from an agricultural to an urban and industrialized society—these general trends were supported or symbolized by specific occurrences, among them the death of Queen Victoria in 1901, the flights of the Wright brothers in 1903, and in 1914 the great climax of the first World War. At the same time, startling new ideas were being promulgated by Carl Jung in anthropology and psychology, by Sigmund Freud in psychology, by William James in philosophy and psychology, by Henri Bergson in philosophy, by Albert Einstein in the sciences, and by Sir James Frazer in anthropology. However little or much the theories of these important thinkers may have been understood by their popular audiences, there can be no question of their impact. For example, Jung's work suggested strange and universal links among all people, an idea supported by Frazer's study of myths which repeat themselves from one community to another, from one culture to another. The explorers offered support for each others' ideas, and the ideas themselves inflamed the curious and sensitive who learned of the new discoveries.

During this period of turmoil and change, old truths were called into question, and certainty was replaced by doubt. In religion and

15

ethics, in politics and social institutions, in philosophy and
aesthetics, tradition was overturned and new answers to eternal
questions were postulated, generally with hesitation, and rarely
with the seeming assurance and optimism which had characterized
the Victorian Age. No longer was the pattern of Victorian family life
acceptable. Young women rebelled at being taught a few graceful
arts or (depending on social position) a domestic skill while awaiting
husbands with demure docility, and young men objected to being
guided or coerced into the army, the church, or a trade at their
parents' behest. The men who went off to the first World War
believing in the heroism and glory of the storytellers found these to
be "old men's lies" and then, "unbelieving," came "home to old lies
and new infamy," as their contemporary, the poet Ezra Pound,
describes. Summarizing his reaction to the waste of the "Great War,"
Pounds speaks for many of these young men and women:

> There died a myriad,
> And of the best, among them,
> For an old bitch gone in the teeth,
> For a botched civilization. [1]

The women who had been left at home also learned the nature of
the lies which society had told them. They found that they were
able to work at offices and in factories; they were able to operate a
typewriter or ride a bicycle; they were able to enter the political life
of the country or enjoy a sexual relationship with a man; they could
think and argue, become educated, and even (in time) vote. Men
and women alike verbalized their questions about the existence of
God and their doubts about the relevance of that question. They
began more frequently to discuss and to experience premarital sex,
unwanted pregnancies, and birth control. After the death of Queen
Victoria, they were freer to speak of flaws in their government. And
consistently they began to doubt, to recognize that uncertainty was
everywhere the norm.

Literature necessarily was affected, for literature cannot help
reflecting the age which produces it. Modernism (the literary movement within which Virginia Woolf is a central figure) takes its name
and its characteristics from the modern age: as the period is marked
by change and uncertainty, so is the literature of the period. In
striving to present the rapid and often disturbing changes in their
world, the writers of this era felt it essential to reform their means of

expression. Poetry, drama, and fiction were subjected to intensive scrutiny and extensive redefinition, producing some of the most unusual and often difficult literary creations in English: Eliot's *Waste Land*, Yeats's *Plays for Dancers*, and the fiction of Joyce and Lawrence are some examples. Modernist literature reflects in its structure as well as in its content the overturning of tradition; the insistence upon new design produced plays and stories without plots or recognizably human characters, poems without rhyme or meter.

It would be difficult for any young person to grow up in such a time without being strongly affected by the persistent doubt, change, and tumult: it was certainly impossible for so sensitive a person as Virginia Stephen, surrounded from her infancy by intelligent, active, probing individuals.[2]

II   *Miss Stephen*

Virginia Stephen's father, a tremendously energetic man, dominated his family's life. He was a parson turned agnostic, a statesman and man of letters who climbed mountains for relaxation. In the year of Virginia's birth, he was editor of the *Cornhill Magazine*, a respected family journal, and he began to compile the *Dictionary of National Biography*, the achievement for which he is best known. Virginia's mother was a gentler person whose large family kept her well occupied. The descriptions which Virginia left of her parents in her novels (they are the main models for the Hilberys in *Night and Day* and the Ramsays in *To The Lighthouse*) suggest that her father offered her a model of intellectual curiosity and power, and gave her an admiration and talent for writing and a love of argument, while her mother reinforced the fanciful and emotional aspects of her nature. She also inherited her mother's beauty. The Stephen home was a gathering place for great ideas and books, and for the great people of the day. Virginia's godfather was James Russell Lowell, American ambassador in London and a poet related to famous literary families in the United States. In this atmosphere the young Virginia had access to an education such as few have known; still she always felt cheated that she was neither sent to the University like her brothers nor expected to perform as they were. She was taught by parents who, though intelligent and educated, lacked the patience of good teachers. But she had access to the contents of her father's extensive library and she read voraciously both there and in the London Library and British

Museum. As she read, Virginia also tried writing, experimenting in different styles and modes, and even, with her brothers and sisters, preparing a family newsletter.[3]

The tenor of life at the Stephen house reflected mixed temperaments and needs. Sir Leslie expected quiet when he wanted it, and quiet is not easily maintained in a home with eight children. When Leslie Stephen married Julia Jackson Duckworth in 1878, it was for each a second marriage. Leslie Stephen's first wife, Minny (the daughter of novelist William Thackeray), died in 1875, leaving him a daughter, Laura, who had inherited her maternal grandmother's insanity and who was eventually institutionalized. His second wife, a widow, brought to their marriage three children: George, Stella, and Gerald Duckworth. To Leslie and Julia Stephen were born four more children: Vanessa, Julian Thoby, Virginia, and Adrian. The four Stephen children were near in age and remained close friends, especially the two sisters, who were united by a mutual interest in art and by their shy awkwardness in the social gatherings into which they were constantly thrust. George, Stella, and Gerald Duckworth were considerably older; Laura, in spite of her madness, lived at home during Virginia's childhood and early adolescence. Tensions necessarily broke into the harmony of a large family with multiple sets of children. Quentin Bell speculates that some of these tensions and specifically Virginia's later nervousness (including her probable frigidity and her mental illness) were caused by the amorous attentions paid to the young girl by her half-brothers, George and Gerald.[4] There was also conflict between the rigid mores of the family's upper-middle class background and the increasing desire for change and freedom among the Stephen children, a desire not shared by the Duckworths. Still, the large family, and especially Vanessa, Adrian, and Thoby, offered Virginia companionship, and her father, whatever his failures in temper and moderation, was her silent comrade on long walks, her mentor and teacher.

Virginia was a contemplative child, although both as a child and later as an adult she had a well-honed sense of humor and could be very mischievous. She learned to talk late, but words were soon to be her forte and her weapon in the nursery competition. Vanessa intended to be the family artist, Virginia the writer, and from early childhood Virginia invented bedtime stories which delighted her brothers and sisters. A sensitive and impressionable child, Virginia was strongly affected by her mother's death in 1895 and by her father's immoderate, rather histrionic mourning. At this time she experienced the first of the series of mental collapses which were to plague her throughout her life and which finally led to her death. Such limited treatment as was available proved efficacious in 1895. But further tragedy was soon to descend upon the Stephens. After their mother's death Virginia's half-sister, Stella, managed the household, postponing marriage until Vanessa was old enough to take over. The joy which her delayed marriage and subsequent pregnancy caused in the Stephen home was quickly stilled by her death in 1897. Soon after Sir Leslie's death in 1904, the four Stephen children moved to a house in Bloomsbury. With this move began a new phase in Virginia's life.

III   *Bloomsbury: The Growth of an Artist*

The period from 1904 to 1911 served as the young writer's apprenticeship and the young woman's maturation. During a second mental and physical breakdown in 1904, Virginia tried to commit suicide by jumping from a window which was, however, not high enough for her to be hurt.[5] She recovered from this breakdown slowly, after a long period of illness. Yet it was at this time that she wrote her first work for publication: a description of her father's relationship with his children, to be included in a biography of Sir Leslie by F. W. Maitland. Late in 1904 her first review article appeared (in a London weekly, *The Guardian*), and one week later her essay describing Haworth Parsonage in Yorkshire was published by the same paper. Thus Virginia Woolf had taken her first professional steps.

By early 1905 she had recovered sufficiently from illness to rejoin her family in the free and unconventional home in Bloomsbury. Here Thoby brought his Cambridge friends for cocoa and conversation, and the shy Virginia and Vanessa gradually learned to enter the discussions of the young college students with a degree of freedom surprising both for them as individuals and for two women at the turn of the century. These were not the boring parties which so frightened the shy Stephen sisters; they were rather the tentative and casual beginnings of what would later be called the Bloomsbury Group. By this time too, Virginia was regularly reviewing books for *The Times Literary Supplement*, and had begun to teach at an evening college for working men and women. The former connection lasted most of her life, providing a fairly steady (if small) income;

the latter was short-lived, for however intelligent and concerned Virginia was, she lacked the teacher's adaptability and ease with people. A trip to Greece was planned in 1906—a grand excursion for the four Stephens, who were accompanied by Violet Dickinson, a long-time friend with whom Virginia was then in love. But on the trip first Vanessa became ill, and later both Violet Dickinson and Thoby contracted typhoid fever, from which Thoby did not recover. Thoby's death was a tremendous loss for Virginia. She wrote about it in her letters and in *Jacob's Room* and *The Waves*. In each novel she describes a young man, shadowy and at best half-known by his acquaintances and the reader: Jacob, whose nature and life must be deduced from the objects in his room, and the silent Percival, who is revealed to us only by the insights and guesses of six of his friends.

Change continued to dominate Virginia's life. In 1907, Vanessa married the artist Clive Bell, and Adrian and Virginia moved nearby to 29 Fitzroy Square. But change was not only personal, for these were years of ferment. To one as interested in aesthetics and artistic experimentation as Virginia Stephen, 1910 was notable for the First Post Impressionist Exhibition, engineered by her friend, Roger Fry. Paintings by Van Gogh, Picasso, Matisse, and others were shown: although many are today recognized masters, their unconventional works shocked the prewar English public, causing an outcry which touched all the Stephens' artistic friends. Meanwhile Virginia continued to practice her writing, and worked on *The Voyage Out*, her first novel, which took seven years to complete. She was not in a hurry to finish the book, and in her desire to achieve as nearly perfect a work as she was capable, she was supported by friends who became known to the world as the Bloomsbury Group.[6]

Beginning in friendships formed by Thoby at Cambridge, the Bloomsbury group gradually grew to include some of the most important creative thinkers and artists of the day. United by a mutual interest in philosophy, literature, and the arts, and by a willingness to shun the conventional in behavior as in thought, these friends represented a wide variety of professions and achievements. Virginia was a journalist and novelist and Vanessa an artist, while Clive Bell was an artist and art critic. Lytton Strachey wanted to write poetry but achieved some fame as a historian and biographer. Leonard Woolf also exhibited the characteristic Bloomsbury variety, for he was a successful civil servant before becoming a politician and author. For Sidney Saxon-Turner music was central; for Roger Fry and Duncan Grant, the visual arts; for Desmond MacCarthy, literary criticism. The more practical fields of mathematics and economics were represented by H. T. J. Norton and John Maynard Keynes, respectively. And this list is not comprehensive: others (including the novelist E. M. Forster) drifted in and out of Bloomsbury. But these formed the nucleus, the constant center.

The Bloomsbury Group did not grow up all at once, nor was it intentionally developed. Woolf, Strachey, and Saxon-Turner were Cambridge friends of Thoby's who formed the earliest Bloomsbury Group in simple get-togethers at the new home of the young Stephens. Although this group quickly dissolved (Leonard Woolf, for example, was in India from 1904 to 1911), it reformed in the teens. The role of geography was far less significant than that of similarity of ideas and interests. The Group traced its ideas to the influence of the philosopher G. E. Moore and his book *Principia Ethica*. In Moore the associates found support for their belief in the ideals of friendship, love, and affection, relationships which could flourish only in an atmosphere of frankness and freedom from prudery. Personal morality and responsibility took the place of conventional mores and socially imposed rules. Communication was a supreme goal which could best be achieved through love and friendship. Where love failed art might succeed. Less intense and less immediate, art was also more enduring. For all of their belief in the power of the intellect and of rational questioning the Bloomsbury associates regarded art with a neo-Romantic mysticism, as a quasi-religion. Accepting that art has a social function, these artists promulgated their religion and promoted art for the masses. But primarily art stood for nothing outside itself and served no other gods. Roger Fry, perhaps the chief theoretician of Bloomsbury, argued that the function of the artist is to find a way of ordering the infinite variety and chaos of nature, and that it is essential for the artist to present his own feelings and view of reality. That is, art is imaginative and emotional, not intellectual, yet it must keep in touch with nature and be guided by the rational side of the artist, so that the emotion finds what Fry and Bell termed "significant form." Thus these artists were devoted to a search for the truth, but a truth of the emotions; they were equally concerned with the form within which that truth could best be expressed. If in that search or in the struggle to create viable forms they shocked their contemporaries by breaking rules, that was a necessary accompaniment, not to be regarded as an evil.

The term "Bloomsbury" may have first been used by Desmond

MacCarthy's wife, and if so was probably invented "for private convenience, not for public mystification" (Pippett, 58). But the public
was aware of the Bloomsbury Group, and because of interlocking
friendships associated the Group with the Post Impressionist Exhibition. Artists too began to attack Bloomsbury, seeing it not as a
collection of friends who enjoyed open exchanges of ideas and
creativity but as an exclusive and pretentious collection of snobbish
Bohemians. Nor were these critics altogether wrong: the members
of the Bloomsbury Group were generally upper-middle class in their
origins and education, delighted in endless intellectual debate
which could be characterized as "highbrow," and followed an "art
for art's sake" credo. Yet they had no single philosophy to impose,
they were not exclusively artists, and even the artists among them
strove to popularize the arts, through workshops and theaters,
public lectures and public service. Many also had related practical
jobs: Fry sold furniture and crafts, David Garnett and Francis
Birrell sold books, and Virginia and Leonard Woolf founded the
Hogarth Press.

By 1911, some members of the Group were beginning to achieve
recognition in their respective fields. But they were all young and in
no rush to find sudden fame; all were innovators searching after
something they called "truth." In their company, the shy Virginia
flourished. However delicate their criticism (in deference to her extreme sensitivity), it was astute; and their support, however tinged
by the complexities of personal interrelationships, was genuine.
Their spirit of free thought encouraged Virginia to develop her own
independence, and their sense of faith in the possibilities of art encouraged her to seek in her own fiction ways to express her vision of
the new world, one which Bloomsbury was helping to define and to
shape.

IV   Mrs. Woolf

In 1912, Virginia Stephen married Leonard Woolf and began
nearly thirty years of a relationship marked by a paradoxical combination of independence and interdependence. Virginia worked
alone, guided by personal values and commitments: after her first
novel no one, not even Leonard, saw or heard anything of what she
wrote until it was finished. Once she finished a novel, she fearfully
sought her friends' reactions. But it was Leonard's approval that
mattered most. Sometimes in her despair at what she considered her

failure, she would ask that he decide if a completed novel should be published or destroyed. All the novels were published, but for Leonard merely evaluting the work must have been a terrible burden: Virginia often seemed to approach insanity as she finished a novel, and more than once she appeared to cross the border into madness. Thus the temptation to praise a work highly regardless of its quality must have been great; yet Leonard knew that for all of her morbid sensitivity to criticism, Virginia respected his judgment and the truth. Throughout their marriage, Leonard was Virginia's protector and nurse. He regulated the hours in which she could write or read, he limited the number of visitors, and he often determined what she should eat and when she should rest. All of this may seem strange when we consider Virginia's independent nature, her talent, and her years of living alone (or with a brother who did not provide such guidance or control). Yet it seemed necessary. Because there were no cures for Virginia's illness and because both Leonard and Virginia felt the stigma attached at that time to mental illness, the need to prevent a breakdown was paramount.

Besides her own references in the *Diary* and the *Letters,* Leonard's description of Virginia's illness is best; he and others called it manic-depressive disease though her own doctors called it neurasthenia.[7] Strain produced symptoms which they learned to recognize as "danger signals": headache, insomnia, rapid pulse, "racing thoughts." She became extremely nervous, unable to concentrate; living, even working—usually "the only way I keep afloat" (AWD, 140)—seemed impossible. Immediate and often prolonged rest, a "vegetative life," might alleviate the symptoms. But on four occasions this did not work, or Virginia was unable to cooperate with the restrictive regimen. Two of these breakdowns have been described above; a third occurred in 1912 - 15 when she finished her first novel; the fourth led to her death by drowning in 1941. During the actual collapse she could not eat or rest, had delusions (once hearing the birds sing in Greek outside her window), could be suicidally depressed or wildly, violently manic, and was unaware that she was ill although when stable she could discuss her disease. It is to Leonard's credit that in spite of his apparent fears about mental illness, he recognized the applicability of the poet Dryden's famous words: "madness is to genius near allied." He considered certifying Virginia, as suicidal patients all were in those days, but he did not, knowing that the gloom of the available asylums and nursing homes could do her no possible good. And he realized that it was impossible for her to lead a quiet and vegetative life, because this would preclude her writing. His assertion that "Virginia's genius was closely connected with what manifested itself as mental instability and insanity" is supported by the creative flights of imagination and fantasy which imbue her novels, as well as by the testimony of her associates. Even Virginia saw her illnesses as somehow "mystical," a time in which her active mind "shuts itself up" and "becomes chrysalis," so that half-formed thoughts and feelings could develop (Bell, II, 149).

Virginia Woolf was not a melancholy person. Leonard describes her as intensely beautiful when happy or excited, but capable of suddenly showing the "anxiety and pain" of fatigue or illness (*Beginning Again*, 28). Acquaintances too recognized this variety in her.[8] She could be shy and awkward in society, or biting and malicious, or fully at ease, graciously making others feel likewise at ease. Her beauty and elegance are consistently noted, but so are her unstylish clothes. She was an energetic person, enjoying long walks in the country or on London's streets, staying up late at parties. Her love of jokes led her to be a tease; her interest in people could turn her curiosity into nosiness; she could lie unhesitatingly. She was witty and a superb conversationalist, but also a fine listener. Nonetheless, those who knew of her illness and even some who did not, consistently remark on an undercurrent of sadness or wistfulness, an occasional withdrawal. Illness limited Virginia's life: she was not allowed to have children, whole months were lost to the limbo of disease, and her writing was restricted in ways which would have defeated a less driven and talented author.

Although Virginia Woolf's first novel, *The Voyage Out*, was completed in 1913, it was not published until 1915 because of her illness and because of the war. Although they escaped direct combat, the Woolfs found the war years difficult: neither could work successfully; Virginia was severely ill, there were financial worries, and of course they shared in the shock that World War I imposed upon everyone. During the war the Woolfs began a project that was to occupy them through much of their lives. From a secondhand printing press bought in 1917 developed first a basement hobby and later Hogarth Press, the publishing house that disseminated some of the writings of E. M. Forster, Dostoevski, Katherine Mansfield, T. S. Eliot, Sigmund Freud, and Maxim Gorki, among others. The Woolfs began the Press with the usual curiosity of authors to learn what happened to their works after they were written—what the processes of printing, binding, and covering were like. Soon they were involved in running a small but active and time-consuming business. For Virginia, reading and selecting manuscripts, setting type, and packing books were sources of genuine pleasure. Those aspects of the work that were purely physical provided much-needed relaxation from mental strain. The Hogarth Press, which drew its name from the Woolf residence in Richmond, published all of Virginia's works after 1917, and also made available the experimental writings of some of the most important authors of the day. Running a business at once aesthetic and practical was typical of the Bloomsbury Group, whose members were rapidly becoming established and gaining recognition at the end of the war. After Lytton Strachey's *Queen Victoria* was published by Harcourt Brace in 1920, that firm became the American publisher for Fry, Forster, and Clive Bell, as well as the Woolfs. For writers who had at first expected to find neither a publisher nor a market, this represented recognition and achievement. Bloomsbury might be offbeat, but it was no longer the home of the struggling young artist.

Virginia Woolf's first novel met with mixed response: perhaps not quite experimental enough for some of her friends, the book was nonetheless not traditional enough for the reading public, especially a public strained by war. In spite of the lukewarm reaction to this novel, Virginia turned almost immediately to a second, *Night and Day*, published in 1919, and to the more experimental work of her short stories, *The Mark on the Wall* (the first issue from the Hogarth Press, in 1917), *Kew Gardens* (1919), and *Monday or Tuesday* (1921; rpt. in *A Haunted House* except for two stories she chose not to retain). At the same time she continued writing and collecting essays and reviews to reflect and develop her aesthetic theories. *The Common Reader: First Series* was published in 1925, but some precepts contained in this series of essays had already been put to work in an earlier novel, *Jacob's Room* (1922). Far more than her previous novels, *Jacob's Room* called forth both strong praise and strong criticism. After this, however, the novels and essays and works less traditionally categorized appeared regularly. Two serious novels, *Mrs. Dalloway* (1925) and *To the Lighthouse* (1927), were followed by the fantasy-history *Orlando* (1928). Similarly, the feminist essay, *A Room of One's Own* (1929), and the difficult but magnificent novel, *The Waves* (1931), led to another change of pace in the *jeu d'esprit*, *Flush* (1933). During those most productive years of the late twenties and early thirties, the *Letter to a Young*

Poet and *The Common Reader: Second Series* were also published, continuing to develop and express their author's theoretical interests. After this, her rate of production slowed, with only two more novels being published—*The Years* in 1937 and *Between the Acts* in 1941. A second feminist work, *Three Guineas*, came out in 1938, and a biography of Roger Fry was published in 1940. The rest of the published books were posthumous, although many of these are collections of earlier writings, including reviews published earlier. Until 1975 only a few of her letters were readily available, some in a collection, *Virginia Woolf and Lytton Strachey: Letters* (1956), and some in the various biographies, but in 1975 the first volume of an extensive collection of letters was published, with five more volumes expected to complete the project in 1980. Similarly, in 1954, Leonard Woolf published excerpts from his wife's extensive diaries, under the title *A Writer's Diary*, and publication of the complete diaries began in 1977.

Writing did not come easily to Virginia Woolf, perhaps because it mattered so much to her. She drove herself to perfection. Her workday was carefully divided: when she was well enough, a few hours each morning would be spent standing at her writing desk or sitting in an armchair in her untidy workroom, producing notebooks filled with a gossamer-thin and often nearly illegible hand; these were her hours of creativity, writing a few pages of the newest novel or perhaps painstakingly revising a single passage from the previous day's work. Afternoons and evenings were devoted to the Press, to reading and walking, to gardening and visiting. Virginia Woolf increasingly became a public figure, a lecturer on literature and women's rights, outspoken against censorship, yet rejecting such formal approbation as honorary degrees. But the joys of writing successfully, of having a few good friends, even the more ambiguous joy of public acclaim were intermingled with pain during the thirties. Her illnesses, both physical and mental, became increasingly problematic, the sharp shifts in her moods increasingly noticeable. A series of deaths, both of friends (including Strachey and Fry) and of a favorite nephew, caused constant pain and reminders of her own precarious grasp on life and on sanity; the rumblings of a second world war in a generation served too as a shadow of death and a reminder of the world's insanity. Bombs destroyed her home in London, and England feared for its survival. Through all of her illnesses, Leonard had been, she declared, "a perfect angel, only more to the point than most angels"; in the same letter she adds, "I should have shot myself long ago in one of these illnesses if it had not been for him" (Pippett, 306). Finally it all became too much for her, and on March 28, 1941, leaving one note for Leonard and another for her sister, she dropped her hat and walking stick on the bank of the River Ouse, walked into the water, and drowned. It is clear that her decision was influenced by the external events noted above. Yet she did not feel that she had no reason to live. Her diaries reveal that on the contrary she thought she had more to say through writing, in additional novels. In fact there exist fragments of an unfinished work, *Anon*, which Quentin Bell describes as "a kind of history of literature" (II, 222).[9] Her letter to Leonard suggests that the fundamental reason for her suicide was her fear of facing another period of illness, perhaps this time to be permanent, and thus of wasting his life as well as hers.[10]

As Virginia Woolf's death suggests the confusion and doubt of the modern age, so her works attempt to give an artistic form to that prevailing sense. But they also offer a tentative alternative in a humanism which may suggest a way of finding value in that unruly world. Virginia Woolf was a representative of modernism, a member of the influential Bloomsbury Group, a woman living in a time of change. But pre-eminently she was an artist, and her legacy is that of the artist: the capturing of what she called her "vision" in language. It is here that our final interest must lie, and it is her aesthetic theories and practice to which we now must turn.

CHAPTER 2

Essays and Criticism

I   The Modern Age

IT is probably an exaggeration to say that the transition from the Victorian to the modern age was as striking as the movement from the Middle Ages to the Renaissance. But the exaggeration is slight, for the change happened far more quickly and created a more notable sense of disorientation. Virginia Woolf perhaps spoke for the writers coming of age around World War I: "We are sharply cut off from our predecessors. A shift in the scale—the sudden slip of masses held in position for ages—has shaken the fabric from top to bottom, alienated us from the past and made us perhaps too vividly conscious of the present" (CE I, 157). With society, self, and universe so shaken, it is not surprising that these writers felt themselves alienated. Nor is the intensity of their awareness of this condition unreasonable.

If Virginia Woolf recognized that she might be overdramatizing the alienation that does not invalidate the awareness itself. All writers are influenced by their surroundings. They work within the codes and values which inform their world and thus shape them, and they document in their works a personal interpretation of that world (their "vision," to use Virginia Woolf's word). Literature is affected by the writer's sense of what contemporary events and values mean, and "reality" may be less significant than the author's perception of reality, his "vision."

To a writer like Virginia Woolf, the fundamental "shift in the scale," the overturning of much that Victorian England had consistently supported, necessitated an attempt first to understand these changes and next to describe them. The need to describe the new vision in turn led her and some of her contemporaries to consider whether the familiar forms of art were adequate. To be sure, there remained important traditional writers: Arnold Bennett, H. G. Wells, and John Galsworthy, for example, attracted wide readership

28

while lesser imitators of these and earlier writers fed an audience especially hungry for fiction. But Virginia Woolf was not alone in her belief that one way to revitalize literature was to change its forms. She was part of a minority, though a minority which matters: with writers like James Joyce, T. S. Eliot, D. H. Lawrence, and W. B. Yeats, she felt she was turning Victorian literature into modern literature. Woolf and the self-conscious modernists exaggerated the disparities between their work and that of their less experimental contemporaries, just as they saw an exaggerated gulf between the nineteenth and twentieth centuries, in terms of reality and sensibility alike. The continuity of Victorian realism and the social and problem novels can be seen in Joyce and Lawrence's work; while, on the other hand, even Bennett, Wells, and Galsworthy (the three whom Woolf sets up as prototypically unmodern) play their part in modern literature.

Because she was a literary critic, a reviewer, a journalist, an essay and pamphlet writer, as well as a novelist, Virginia Woolf left a published record of her aesthetic views. Because she enjoyed reading and thought about what she read, she also frequently wrote her opinions of other authors in her diary. She has not left an orderly record: rather, we must search through diaries, essays, letters, and novels for evidence of her beliefs. Her comments about the work of other writers suggest something of her values and her feelings about art. As she discusses her own writing she reveals her dedication to the struggle to create art. Occasionally her diary entries and essays directly confront theoretical questions about literature. Her best criticism comes in discussing individual works, for her response is subtle and her mind alert. Her pronouncements about matters of theory are frequently less satisfactory, as she tends to be both impressionistic and dogmatic, a dangerous combination. To study Virginia Woolf's criticism is to study modernism and its attempt once again to define the functions of art.

II *Art in an Age of Doubt*

The vision of the modernists is characterized by questioning and uncertainty. "Why," Virginia Woolf asks, should life seem "so like a little strip of pavement over an abyss"? (AWD, 27). She may decry the pessimism of the Russian novelists as one-sided (CE II, 109 - 10), but like many others she felt her world balanced precariously over a bottomless chasm. In an important essay on the

art of modern fiction, "Mr. Bennett and Mrs. Brown," Virginia
Woolf observes that human relations have changed significantly in
her lifetime, and "when human relations change there is at the
same time a change in religion, conduct, politics, and literature."
She dates this significantly though facetiously at the year of the Post
Impressionist Exhibition, asserting that "in or about December,
1910, human character changed" (CE I, 320). The very sense of
what it means to be an individual had been profoundly affected.
The explorations into the nature of human life and relations led the
modernists to ask who they were, or what a person is, or how we are
all related. And from these questions come the artist's twin concerns: whether a fictitious person, a character in a novel or play or
poem, might be described, and if so, how.

   To Virginia Woolf the individual is infinitely complex. There are
no clear boundaries between one person and the next, or between
one's past, present, and future. Into each person, Virginia Woolf ex-
claims, "nature . . . let creep instincts and desires which are utterly
at variance with his main being, so that we are streaked, variegated,
all of a mixture; the colours have run." The single identity we
appear at any given moment may not be the "true self"; it is only
"for convenience" that we unite the "wandering facets of our multiple selves" (CE IV, 161). The reader who is aware of the modernist temper will not be surprised to find that Virginia Woolf sees life
itself as shifting and flowing, contradictory and unstable.

   In several essays, most notably *A Room of One's Own*, "How It
Strikes a Contemporary," and "The Leaning Tower," Virginia
Woolf argues that the artist needs peace, security, leisure, and
financial independence, as well as the solid education which these
four would permit. Before World War I, she suggests, these were
routinely available for most potential artists or at least for most male
artists. After 1914 the ivory towers of the upper-middle class and its
educational institutions were "no longer steady towers. They were
leaning towers." Artists struggled to write amidst change and the
threat of war, pitied themselves, and directed their anger against
the society which allowed such discomfort to exist (CE II, 166 - 77).
The conditions of disorientation and dislocation were real enough.
The First World War touched every aspect of human life, including
human relations. The light of gunfire clarified vision, so that
"romance was killed": "so ugly they looked—German, English,
French—so stupid" (*Room*, 15). The same light was shed on earlier
truths, and artists no longer believed what they had been taught

What is true and enduring is "the spirit," she argues,
materialists disappoint us with their concern for "the
le they may be fine craftsmen, "life escapes" them, the
matters to *her* is lost. That "essential thing" the earlier
failed to capture is defined in images which continue to
egularly by students of modern literature:

n and life, it seems, is very far from being 'like this'. Examine
t an ordinary mind on an ordinary day. The mind receives a
essions—trivial, fantastic, evanescent, or engraved with the
steel. From all sides they come, an incessant shower of in-
oms; and as they fall, as they shape themselves into the life of
uesday, the accent falls differently from of old; the moment of
ame not here but there; so that, if a writer were a free man
ve, if he could write what he chose, not what he must, if he
is work upon his own feeling and not upon convention, there
plot, no comedy, no tragedy, no love interest or catastrophe in
style, and perhaps not a single button sewn on as the Bond
would have it. Life is not a series of gig-lamps symmetrically
is a luminous halo, a semi-transparent envelope surrounding
eginning of consciousness to the end. (CE II, 106)

true, she continues, isn't it necessary for the writer "to
varying, this unknown and uncircumscribed spirit,"
o so he must abandon the traditions and disappoint the
pectations? She is not merely seeking "courage and
she explains, but suggesting that the "proper stuff" of
not what we have been led to believe (CE II, 105 - 106).
ticism and novels Virginia Woolf presents her own
st to define and then to convey the modern world view.
r constant emphasis on looking inward to "the dark
sychology" (CE II, 108) it is not surprising to find that
Virginia Woolf's criticism is a concern with character.
aracter is especially important to the novelist, her com-
oncerned with more than the art of fiction. For example,
Gibbon as a historian because he does not merely pre-
but is also "the critic and the historian of the mind" (CE
Vhatever else may constitute the "proper stuff" of
t is clear that to Virginia Woolf people (characters) are

are often driven to write novels, she argues, because they
on to create some character which has . . . imposed itself

and what their predecessors had written about. It seemed to them
that they could write only from direct experience, that their own
senses and emotions were more reliable than their intellects. Rather
than stories which they could not believe, they produced fragments,
"not books but notebooks," jottings from which later generations of
artists might be able to make works of more apparent or lasting
value (CE II, 159 - 60).

Such notebooks record experimentation and hard work as the artists struggle to express their new vision of man and his world.
Virginia Woolf repeatedly characterizes modernism and its
literature as being alive to change: "No age of literature is so little
submissive to authority as ours, so free from the dominion of the
great; none seems so wayward with its gift of reverence, or so
volatile in its experiments" (CE II, 38 - 39). It is hard to cut new
paths through dense woods, and often discouraging to watch others
walk with apparent ease over the worn routes. In "The Narrow
Bridge of Art," Virginia Woolf argues that art no longer serves the
modern writers as it has their predecessors, because "the mind is
full of monstrous, hybrid, unmanageable emotions. That the age of
the earth is 3,000,000,000 years; that human life lasts but a second;
that the capacity of the human mind is nevertheless boundless; that
life is infinitely beautiful yet repulsive; that one's fellow creatures
are adorable but disgusting; that science and religion have between
them destroyed belief; . . . it is in this atmosphere of doubt and
conflict that writers have now to create" (CE II, 219). Her exaggeration may be annoying, since writers of many periods have experienced alienation or loss of belief, but it is typical of her time.

In the attempt to create the writer should feel bound neither by
convention nor by tradition. "Any method is right, every method is
right," Virginia Woolf asserts in defense of experimental literature
(CE II, 108). Yet her essays, reviews, and diary reveal that she held
some strong and consistent views about what art should be and
about the forms of literature. No critic can come to literature
without some sense of an ideal. One of Virginia Woolf's strengths as
a critic is her receptivity to different kinds of writing. She makes
personal judgments, of course—she did not like *Ulysses*, she
preferred Tolstoi to Dickens. In the muddle of her world she can
still discriminate; she is determined to hold up each novel, play, or
poem to the light of the ideal, but she does so with a cautious and
open mind.

III   Is "Every Method . . . Right"?

Are there eternal principles about what art is or about what makes a given work of art a "masterpiece"? Although Virginia Woolf is well aware of the influence of time and place on readers and critics as well as on writers, she seems also to suggest, however cautiously, a positive answer to those questions. It may be that the Russian novel differs from the English in method and point-of-view as well as in the specific details of history or geography, or that the Elizabethan and Victorian audiences each expected something different in their art, and neither wanted what a modern audience might. But there are certain qualities we expect in all writing, or all that we call good.

Because she believes that the critic should "seize upon what is good . . . and expatiate upon that" (CW 77 - 78), Virginia Woolf in her specific criticism reveals what she values in art. "Writing is always difficult" (AWD, 25, cf. 196); that is, it *is* an art, not a natural activity but one that is learned and developed. The writer's central idea will be of interest and significance only if it is personal, sufficiently encompassing, and profound; "vision" and characters alike must reveal his sensitivity, humor, intelligence, and knowledge. But these are not enough. The whole work must be unified, well written, interesting in style as well as in content. Only then can this be a work that will affect us in the best manner, stimulating our minds and arousing our sympathetic emotional response. The words of praise which she chooses reveal these priorities even as they display her reliance on a tradition of imprecise, impressionistic criticism: "alight with intelligence" (CE I, 349); "clean cut, decisive, masterly, hard as rock"; "admirable economy and sharpness of stroke"; "the lucidity, the ease, the power of the words" (CE I, 353); "an exquisite discrimination of human values"; "likeness to life," "wit," and "taste" (CE I, 148 - 50)—all these will create art which "excites" and "moves" and "changes" us (CE I, 354).

Although Virginia Woolf does not disdain escape literature ("rubbish-reading"), she argues that a great work of art appeals to more than our desire to be entertained (CE I, 21). More aspects of a person are "roused and brought into action" in proportion to the quality of the work (CE I, 14). The responsibility is not wholly the artist's, for an inadequate reader may not respond properly to even the greatest novel or poem. Only by putting bias aside can the

reader see from the author's poi
perspective (CE I, 34, 70 - 71).
from preconceptions about what
(CE II, 1 - 2). If we feel that esc
quately to our own minds, imag
willing to expend the effort nee
more significant works, not mere
in a good tale (CE I, 3 - 10).

The best literature makes its a
new scenes, other people, and ot
idea or place with new insight, so
new ways. Such literature main
reality. Virginia Woolf suggests
"bore us" when they transmute
distant from our own: "their Sm
Liverpools to fabulous islands a
Literature "must somehow be b
must maintain contact with real
"take off into whatever heights it
reveals a writer's genius than hi
fantastic into touch. If literature
while retaining its inherent tru
aginations. In *A Room of One's (*
like a spider's web, attached ev
tached to life at all four corners"

What is this "reality" which
means different things at variou
is that of the early modern perio
bringing, the new ideas about ps
of world war. Thus she praises
"deeper and more hidden emotio
"superficial" one who fails to go
most important aesthetic pronou
tion," Virginia Woolf defines in
She takes to task her undaring
Bennett, Wells, and Galsworth
somewhat exaggerates their ch
detail and perhaps inadequately
creating convincing characters as
important things; that they sper
dustry making the trivial and the

enduring.
but says
body." W
reality th
writers ha
be quoted

Look wi
for a mom
myriad im
sharpness
numerable
Monday o
importance
and not a
could base
would be
the accept
Street tailo
arranged;
us from the

If this
convey th
even if to
reader's
sincerity,
literature
In her c
attempts
With h
places of
central to
Though c
ments are
she praise
sent even
I, 118).
literature,
central.
Authors
are "lured

upon them" (CE I, 319). What must these characters be
Characters must think and feel as well as act, or we cannot tru.., ~~be~~
said to know them (CE I, 141 - 43). They must appear real (CE I,
227), "living men and women" who are individualized, not just
types (CE I, 236; cf. CW 35). It is the "power" of the best novelist
to convince us that "his characters are fellow-beings driven by their
own passions and idiosyncracies, while they have—and this is the
poet's gift—something symbolical about them which is common to
us all" (CE I, 261). In spite of "the inexpressible fineness" of
Milton's style, for instance, Virginia Woolf regrets his lack of em-
pathy: "I scarcely feel that Milton lived or knew men and women"
(AWD, 5). A good story is a source of pleasure but the primary purpose of plot is to enhance the reality and significance of the
characters (CE I, 77). In suggesting in a review of a novel that the
adventures of the heroine are "much more interesting than the
heroine herself," she knows she is thus "recommending the book to
half the reading public and condemning it in the eyes of the other
half" (CW 82). Because multi-dimensional characters will not con-
form to social or literary traditions, they create problems for their
authors, but these are risks which authors must be willing to face
and which readers must encourage authors to take (CW 115 - 16).
Characters need to be multi-dimensional because that is what people are.[1] Every nuance of each human complexity is the legitimate
concern of the artist. External details are not enough; the reality
which matters is the inner being only partially revealed by what a
person wears or says or does, however difficult it is to define or capture this reality in ink.

The presentation must be marked by depth of thought and feeling. While she appreciates the spirit of life which pervades the
novels of Charles Dickens, Virginia Woolf feels that his work is
finally "monotonous" since it does not contain "mind," the sensitive perception which is "suggestive" for the reader (AWD, 300 -
02). Yet only if the author maintains contact with the world can he
achieve the necessary scope (CE II, 230 - 31). Thus, unlike Dickens,
Elizabeth Barrett Browning was limited as an artist because her
secluded life forced her to speculate about the world outside and to
magnify that within (CE I, 214). The isolated artist will be finally as
incapable of understanding himself as he will his society (cf. CE I,
233 - 34). In contrast, the fiction of a writer like Turgenev is marked
by "balance" and breadth, because Turgenev was able to escape his
personal and cultural biases (CE I, 249 - 53). At worst, she asserts,

[margin handwritten: power of projecting one's personality into their work.]

literature can be totally ruined by "the damned egotistical self"
which narrows the interests, themes, situations, and people of a
book to reflections of the author (AWD, 22). Yet she condemns
equally one converse of a work with no intellectual interest, that is,
becoming partisan or using literature as propaganda.[2] She argues
that the best literature reflects not only mind but heart—the deep
feelings of a sympathetic and sensitive writer. The author tries to
arouse the reader's emotional response by involving him in the lives
or feelings of the characters in a play or novel, the persona of a
poem.

Finally, the whole work—the author's conception of reality, his
characters, his theme as well as his method of presentation—must
be marked by originality. Art should either present something new
or revitalize the old and familiar. Literature should reflect (and
enhance) life, not other literature. The reviews in *Contemporary
Writers* distinguish originality as a main attribute of an important
work. For instance she complains that one author's failure to make
her "romance" seem real stems from the fact that "her sense of it is
more conventional than original. She has taken it from poetry rather
than from life" (CW 123, cf. 50 - 53). Perhaps it is significant that
this criterion appears so frequently in critiques of her contemporaries, for Virginia Woolf was especially aware of the need for
literature constantly to grow and change. But she values originality
at all times, praising writers as different as Laurence Sterne,
Charlotte Brontë, and Henry James for being unique (CE I, 95,
187 - 88, 283). She is aware of the dangers to which originality can
lead, and of its limitations. Thus she speaks with awe of the risks
which Sterne dared in writing the experimental novel, *Tristram
Shandy*, and of the art required to control the apparent disorder of
his *Sentimental Journey* (CE I, 95 - 96). Still, while originality may
ensure some kind of immediate interest, it does not confer
automatic success. Virginia Woolf is not so concerned with change
and experiment as to be blinded by them. She knows that too much
ingenuity can be pretentious, that "a first-rate writer . . . respects
writing too much to be tricky" or to do "stunts" (AWD, 48; cf. 38 -
39). But the risks must be taken. For example, though she
recognizes weaknesses in her contemporary Dorothy Richardson's
experimental fiction, Virginia Woolf still credits her with a genuine
attempt at presenting something new in an honest way. Richardson's method calls attention to itself—one of the disadvantages of
discarding the norm—but it is not employed out of mere "perver-

sity." "It represents a genuine conviction of the discrepancy between what she has to say and the form provided by tradition for her to say it in" (CW 120).

Virginia Woolf's comments about Dorothy Richardson show that she believes originality must be displayed in form as well as content. It is possible that new ideas may best be expressed in new structures. Her concern with how one says what one says marks Virginia Woolf as a writer and theoretician, and as a modernist. Form and meaning cannot be theoretically separated. No matter how accurate a paraphrase may be, it differs even in "meaning" from the original work. The words and structure of a poem, play, or story are integral to impact and meaning alike; alter the first elements and the second are likewise altered (CE I, 7). If this is a problem within a given language, it becomes insurmountable in translation. As a translator, Virginia Woolf believed that a really good translation was beyond possibility, because the original images, word choice, rhetorical devices, and sentence structure could not be conveyed in another language (CE I, 1 - 13). Not only is translation "literature stripped of its style," but like paraphrase, it is literature whose meaning has been tampered with (CE I, 238 - 39).

Technique is so important to Virginia Woolf that, she reveals, she often first imagines some particular form from which develops an appropriate theme and characters.[3] In spite of the importance of the topic, Woolf's definition of form is vague and unsatisfactory. Objecting to the critic Percy Lubbock's separation of "form" and "the book itself," she says, "When we speak of form we mean that certain emotions have been placed in the right relations to each other." Yet she knows that to discuss specific devices, form and content must be temporarily separated. The novelist places emotions "in the right relations" by employing a variety of methods, some of which he "inherits," others of which he "bends," and still others he "invents for himself" (CE II, 124 - 29).[4]

The successful writer is a careful craftsman who searches for the right word and the right structure, who desires to achieve unity and consistency in his creation (AWD, 67: "The art must be respected"). The critic of literature, whether prose or poetry, must direct his attention to language. Thus Virginia Woolf objects to E. M. Forster's *Aspects of the Novel* because it manifests so little concern with art as art: "almost nothing is said about words" and little about sentence structure or other features of language. It is ironic, and perhaps pathetic, that in such "a wise and brilliant book" as this the artist's medium is granted only "a sentence or two" (CE II, 54). One reason why critics can so easily disregard questions of style is the disparaging attitude of too many prose writers toward their medium. Tending to regard prose "as a humble beast of burden" with which to convey a message or present an argument, they may fail to write with the care of a poet, with the same alertness to sound, the same attempts to vary the length of the sentence and its order. But prose, like poetry, is an art, and writing either is a discipline (CE IV, 1 - 3).

As—according to Woolf—the writer should avoid the immediately available stock words and phrases (CE I, 139 - 40), so he should avoid automatic use of the traditions of his genre. When literary devices call attention to themselves they may make a reader uneasy (CE I, 16); the familiar is more acceptable. But the conventions of any form are restrictive; in fiction, for example, one scene must follow another, "the story has to be finished: the intrigue discovered, the guilty punished, the lovers married in the end" (CE II, 63; cf. CE I, 5, 56). Ideally the artist should be constrained by no more than "a few trifling rules of grammar and spelling"; he should freely alter, discard, or create tradition anew (CE II, 250).

In her diary, Virginia Woolf often speaks of her own writing: what she hopes or wants to do, what she is currently working on, how she evaluates her past creations. When a book seems to her to be "mature and finished and satisfactory" or when she can judge that it seems characterized by "originality and sincerity," she is pleased (AWD, 10). She suggests that her "interest as a writer lies . . . in some queer individuality; not in strength, or passion, or anything startling" (AWD, 43 - 44). Her "reaction is not the usual"; her work is distinguished by a drive to "explore," whether it be characters, ideas, or styles (AWD, 133 - 34). Capable of self-evaluation, she can note possible limitations, such as the thinness of her work or its lack of plot, or the fact that she avoids (or cannot present) substantive reality, perhaps investing her fiction with too little sense of the physical (AWD, 114, 55 - 57). To what extent these are limitations (or even accurate assessments) must be decided as each novel is read. She is not always consistent in her evaluations, because both her ideas about art and her moods change, sometimes abruptly. But Virginia Woolf is always aware of her writing as art and always conscious of an audience. Even when writing in her diary she asks, "Do I ever write, even here, for my own eye?" (276). As encouraged as she could be by a positive review, a friend's

praise, or her own sense of achievement, still she nearly always felt
dissatisfied with her work. When despondent she could assert, "I
shall never write a book that is an entire success" (AWD, 52). But
what she meant by "success" here must be considered: presumably
no artist could ever hope to please self, friends, and critics, and also
write a best seller with lasting significance.

What gave her a greater degree of satisfaction about her work
than almost anything else was the sense that she had for once
managed to project her vision fully, in a form that did it justice.
This sense and the accompanying pleasure were short-lived, for she
would soon be off on another task, struggling again with seemingly
insurmountable problems. Her criticism also reflects her preoccupa-
tion with the artist's search for appropriate form, whether she is
concerned with a nineteenth-century poet like Byron (who, in *Don
Juan*, found an appropriately "elastic shape"—AWD, 3), or the innovative "novel-poem," *Aurora Leigh*, by Elizabeth Barrett Browning (CE I, 214 - 8), or the work of a contemporary like Joseph
Conrad (CE I, 310). It is in the field of modern literature, however,
that she most emphasizes the need for change and growth, because
of an obsession with change and because this is the literature she
was writing. Some "powerful and unscrupulous tyrant" constrains
the traditional writer "to provide a plot, to provide comedy,
tragedy, love interest, and an air of probability," so that if the
characters were "to come to life they would find themselves dressed
down to the last button of their coats in the fashion of the hour. The
tyrant is obeyed; the novel is done to a turn. But sometimes, more
and more often as time goes by, we suspect a momentary doubt, a
spasm of rebellion, as the pages fill themselves in the customary
way. Is life like this?" If life is not "like this," as she strongly urges
us to believe, then the modern writer needs to reevaluate the conventions of literature. Only then can he ever hope to succeed in his
"attempt to come closer to life, and to preserve more sincerely and
exactly what interests and moves" him. For the modern artist, "the
accent falls a little differently; the emphasis is upon something
hitherto ignored"; the changes are "difficult for us to grasp" and
"incomprehensible to our predecessors" but they are necessary (CE
II, 106 - 108). Such insistence makes it obvious that Virginia Woolf
had chosen not to be constrained by the traditional boundaries of
any genre. What those boundaries are or should be, how they can
be widened or discarded, what a play or a poem or especially a
novel really is, are the central questions. Because she truly explores

such questions and because she believes that literature constantly changes, she offers different answers at different times.

IV   The Question of Genre and the Future of Art

Traditionally plays, poems, essays, and stories have been markedly different, distinguished by agreed-upon characteristics. Essays are more factual than stories; poems are so shaped that they look different on paper from essays; plays are to be performed, novels to be read; poems are short and novels long. But even this brief a list is obviously flawed. For example, if poetry is short but in verse while the novel is a prose narrative form, what is a long verse narrative such as *The Odyssey, The Iliad,* or *Paradise Lost?* If plays are to be performed, what is the place of that drama (often in verse) which is far better read than presented on a stage? Recent experimentation has further complicated the situation. Journalistic novels and anti-novels, prose poems, concrete poetry, and computer poetry are just further manifestations of the increased resistance to the usual categories. Virginia Woolf is like many of her contemporaries in needing to redefine her medium to suit the modern world, but she is also like all artists in needing to establish methods to suit herself.

Most of Virginia Woolf's definitions of genre occur indirectly, almost always in the context of a critical review of a specific work, and usually in comparative terms. She differentiates between prose and poetry, drama and fiction, fiction and biography rather than making pronouncements about what each of these should be. It is not surprising that she stresses the impossibility of stating absolute definitions of the various genres and the undesirability of limiting the artist's freedom to experiment as much as he wants to or can.

Poetry and prose, she observes in an essay on De Quincey's prose style, are generally considered separate, each with a different "mission." But by maintaining clear divisions between their work and poetry, prose writers ignore the "rhapsodies" and "dreams" of "that side of the mind which is exposed in solitude." The more courageous writer who experiments with the language of his work has (even in failure) served art by "enlarging and fertilizing and influencing" style. De Quincey was one such writer, who brought into his prose the "fire" and "concentration" of poetry, and its symbolizing ability (CE I, 165 - 72). She argues that poetry tends to generalize, to turn characters from individuals into abstractions or passions, while prose is more likely to dissect and to analyze (CE I, 229). Such tendencies, though, are only that, not absolutes.

Even when discussing the essay—the form of creative prose most dependent upon fact—Virginia Woolf emphasizes artistry. She suggests that in the most successful essays, facts are subsumed into the texture of the writing so that while abundant they are not disruptive (CE II, 41 - 45). Without being obtrusive, an author can make an essay personal. A sufficiently colloquial style will lead the reader to feel that the essayist *is* an individual, someone with whom the reader engages in a kind of conversation (CE II, 46 - 47). Like the essayist, the biographer benefits from the "indisputable power" of facts (CE III, 87), although his genre limits him to selecting, evaluating, and ordering. In contrast the fictitious character "lives in a free world where the facts are verified by one person only—the artist himself," who through his "vision" creates a world which is "rarer, intenser, and more wholly of a piece than the world that is largely made of authentic information supplied by other people." The ideal biography might well be a book which mixed the two kinds of "facts," those historically verifiable and those of the author's vision, but this would require as subject a person about whom relatively little is known, so that the author had relatively more freedom (CE IV, 221 - 28; cf. 229 - 35).

"The play is poetry . . . and the novel prose," Virginia Woolf writes in an essay on Elizabethan drama which analyzes "the prime differences" between drama and fiction. The novel is characterized as being "leisurely" and "accumulated," the play in contrast is "little" and "contracted," with a high degree of immediacy; in the novel, the emotion is "split up," only "gradually" building to "a whole," while in the play it is "concentrated, generalized, heightened"; the playwright presents "the extremes of passion" in typical and representative characters while the novelist focuses on the individual. These differences should not create disappointment in the reader—that the novel, for instance, tends not to deal in the abstract and symbolic—but rather should lead the reader to recognize literature's "inexhaustible richness' (CE I, 58 - 59). If this awareness leads the reader (like Virginia Woolf) into apparent contradictions it also makes him freer to read (or to write) literature which is not limited by the traditional "rules" of each genre.

In *A Writer's Diary* Virginia Woolf underscores the expansion of the traditional genres by proposing new names for some of her "novels," including "elegy," "psychological poem," "biography," "play-poem," "autobiography," and "essay-novel." She notes that as she writes "little bits of rhyme come in" (122) or that she is tempted to "invent a new kind of play . . . away from facts; free;

yet concentrated; prose yet poetry; a novel and a play" (103). Finally she claims that in writing her next-to-last novel she learns all "kinds of 'forms' " can be combined in one book (215). It might be difficult to combine "satire, comedy, poetry, narrative" (191) or "poem, reality, comedy, play; narrative, psychology" (215), but it is possible. In fact, the struggle to find a way to unite the various strands seems to have been among the joys of Virginia Woolf's life (191).

All genres matter; all have the potential to grow. But for Virginia Woolf, the novel matters most. In part this is simply because she is a novelist, but she offers a theoretical defense of her position in essays like "The Narrow Bridge of Art." The novel, being relatively younger, freer, more flexible, demonstrably congenial to experimentation, is a natural vehicle for change. Virginia Woolf may hesitate to define the future of a genre which is undergoing so rapid a transformation (CE II, 97 - 98; CE I, 218), but she has tremendous faith in its potential. "It may be possible that prose is going to take over—has, indeed, already taken over—some of the duties which were once discharged by poetry": "in ten or fifteen years' time prose will be used for purposes for which prose has never been used before. That cannibal, the novel, which has devoured so many forms of art will by then have devoured even more." A new genre based on the novel may come into being: "This book which we see on the horizon may serve to express some of those feelings which seem at the moment to be balked by poetry pure and simple and to find the drama equally inhospitable to them." Like poetry this new novel will give "the outline rather than the detail." It will focus on emotions and thoughts and on the relation between the mind and abstractions. Thus it will satisfy the modern readers' longing "for ideas, for dreams, for imagination" (CE II, 224 - 29; cf. 101 - 102).

How can such a novel be created? Virginia Woolf's fiction offers more interesting if less direct answers, but her theoretical assertions are also of interest. In "Phases of Fiction" she observes the constancy of the "human element" in fiction: novels arouse in us the same feelings that people in real life do. If this is true, then necessarily fiction must retain some grasp on "ordinary things," the realistic surface. But these very features which characterize the novel are "incompatible with design and order. It is the gift of style, arrangement, construction, to put us at a distance from life and obliterate its features; while it is the gift of the novel to bring us into close touch with life." To achieve "balance" between these extremes is the gift of the best novelist (CE II, 99 - 101).

The need for novelists to transform themselves from "materialists" to what she called "spiritualists," to free themselves of the shackles of convention (what in "Modern Fiction" she symbolizes as the compulsion to dress one's characters in the designs of the Bond Street tailors), is a theme Virginia Woolf continues in another major statement, "Mr. Bennett and Mrs. Brown." In this essay, she relates a simple tale of a woman (Mrs. Brown) sitting on a train with a companion, and potentially being observed by Bennett, Galsworthy, Wells, and Woolf herself. Because she believes that the "clumsy, verbose, and undramatic . . . rich, elastic, and alive" form of fiction developed precisely to present characters, Virginia Woolf, seeing "Mrs. Brown," begins to weave a story about her, imagining her relationships with her companion, picturing her in various scenes. On the other hand if the utopianist Wells saw Mrs. Brown, he would immediately envision a better world, while Galsworthy would define her social status and the conditions in which she lives, and Bennett with his interest in external detail would describe the carriage in which she is riding. These three novelists, Woolf argues, look not at Mrs. Brown but at her surroundings: "They have looked very powerfully, searchingly, and sympathetically out of the window . . . but never at her, never at life, never at human nature." As a result, the conventions they used are "ruin" and their "tools are death" for writers like Virginia Woolf. Writers like these "have laid an enormous stress upon the fabric of things. They have given us a house in the hope that we may be able to deduce the human beings who live there." But "if you hold that novels are in the first place about people, and only in the second about the houses they live in, that is the wrong way to set about it." At first, she continues, her contemporaries tried to employ the older methods, attempting "to compromise," integrating their sense of the unique significance of some character with the older writers' sense of external reality. But in doing so they left Mrs. Brown sitting unexamined on the train, and it is Mrs. Brown that they are determined to rescue, "at whatever cost to life, limb, and damage to valuable property" (an only partly jocular assertion). That is why the old methods must be destroyed. "All round us," in all forms of art and writing, she hears "the sound of breaking and falling, crashing and destruction." Progress should derive from this carnage, and when Virginia Woolf vows "never, never to desert Mrs. Brown" it is not only out of conviction: she finds the process of development (even the process of destruction) exhilarating (CE I, 321 - 34).

V   Virginia Woolf as Critic

The best literary criticism, according to Virginia Woolf, offers a
fair and careful analysis, and is well written, informative, and
stimulating. Good criticism makes us want to read literature and
teaches us to be better readers. In fact she warns that the best critic,
the one who helps us to "love poetry," must be "sufficiently gifted"
to be a creative writer himself (CE I, 316). In large measure
Virginia Woolf succeeds in being such a critic. As a writer she is sensitive to the difficulties which other writers face, yet her sympathy
never leads her to offer unnecessary excuses for their failures. The
ideals she establishes for others are no more demanding than those
she sets for herself, and often less so. She is quick to praise the in-
novator, slow to unleash her scorn on lesser writers. But she is
capable of fine and biting judgments. And through her lively, imaginative essays she does capture the reader's interest not only in
her writing but also in the work she is reviewing. She can lead us to
love literature.

Although she can be scrupulously analytic, her normal methods
of literary criticism are unusually creative. Typically (and this is
most true of the literary and biographical sketches in the third and
fourth volumes of the *Collected Essays*) she moves freely between
fact and imagination or impression. To give a historical description
of a selected author, she draws upon the evidence of biographies,
diaries, and letters as well as the author's fiction or poetry. But she
goes beyond data collecting to conjecture about her subject's
probable thoughts and feelings. Sometimes the sketches involve a
great deal of imaginative reconstruction, if the subject is one about
whom little is known or who never lived but might serve as a type
she wishes to describe. For example, she creates in *A Room of One's
Own* a fictitious "sister" of Shakespeare's who can stand for any
woman prevented from becoming an author by social conditions
and expectations. Or she fabricates a scene of an evening in Sir
Walter Scott's life, based only loosely on his Journal (CE I, 134 -
39). But she is equally capable of more objective analysis, whether
dealing with abstractions and absolutes or discussing the effects of
particular lines and words. Thus, for instance, in an essay on John
Donne she wanders freely from considerations of specific phrases in
his poems or more general observations about his style to discussions of the poems' attitudes about love or aspects of the poet's
life (CE I, 32 - 45). Often in her work we are made aware of a quali-

ty which more critics would do well to display: the ability to judge each author and each piece of creative writing on its own terms. This is what allows her appreciatively to discuss Elizabethan plays, John Donne's poems, the novels of nineteenth-century Russians, or the American author Henry James. She was not always so objective about her contemporaries, as one of them—E. M. Forster—notes.[5] She brings to each work her own values (which affect her attitudes toward specific themes or characters) and a sense of appropriate form and style, but she is able to put these aside to a far greater degree than most and thus to evaluate more sensibly. She *can* be opinionated and dogmatic, but often this is purposeful—and sometimes it is a pose. She asserts an absolute rule (novels begin with characters, novels begin with form . . .) only to contradict it later, until we recognize that each absolute is a partial expression of the truth as she sees it. She sets up Bennett and Wells, or Forster, as straw men, for the sake of her argument. Her critical method is not primarily objective and analytic in nature but rather subjective, metaphoric, and rhetorical.

Virginia Woolf's theoretical pronouncements have special importance for those interested in her fiction or in modernism. She is simply a fine critic—sensitive, cogent, balanced, and just. After more than half a century her essays continue to reveal a grace of writing, a clarity of argument, and a rare and wonderful depth of insight, all of which makes them appealing even to readers not attracted by her novels.

CHAPTER 3

Beginnings

"Is life very shifting or very solid?" (AWD, 138).

"Where does she begin, and where do I end?" (*The Years*, 334).

"Broken asunder, yet made in the same mould, could it be that each completed what was dormant in the other?" (*Flush*, 17).

"I think I am the field, I am the barn, I am the trees; . . . I am the seasons" (*The Waves*, 97 - 98).

"Does everything then come over again a little differently? . . . is there a pattern; a theme, recurring like music; half remembered, half foreseen?" (*The Years*, 269).

Repeatedly Virginia Woolf's characters and Virginia Woolf herself ask questions, questions which are haunting because they extend to the fundamental level of human existence. What these fictional men and women want to know are the same things thinking people of all times have asked. But these "questions" are usually grammatically transformed statements asserting that life is complex and that there are no answers. The rhetoric (the fact that the question form is used) thus reiterates the speaker's state of mind. The traditional solutions to the age old dilemmas of human life (what is man? why is he on earth? how should he behave?) are denied directly and vehemently. New answers are tentatively proposed, but rarely do they satisfy the questioner, the author, or even the reader for more than a brief time. The very act of questioning becomes a major mode of thinking in Virginia Woolf's novels. This is not to say that she is cynical or even persistently a skeptic. She is discontented with the obvious, constantly in search of new answers, and willing to discard prior ideas in her open-minded search for understanding. Her rhetoric of discovery is epitomized by the following question and its "answer" from a major novel: "What does the central shadow hold? Something? Nothing? I do not know" (*The Waves*, 379). Such despair is not typical of Virginia Woolf or of the majority of her characters, though the uncertainty is. Her questions arise in three areas: human nature, or the question of identity; the external world, time, and nature, or the question of reality; and human behavior, or the question of values.

What does it mean to be a person? How is any individual related to others—friends, acquaintances, strangers who walk past on the street or who share a bench on the bus, ancestors and descendants (direct or merely genetic—that is, of the human race)? What are the boundaries of identity: how does a person know what makes him or her distinct, what belongs to him, what is a part of nature or of another's identity? How many selves does any person have, and how are they integrated so that they exist in balance and order (if they do)? Questions like these are fundamental to the first area of concern, and recur in all of Virginia Woolf's writings.

When reaching out to touch something tangible and solid—a stone wall, a hard mattress, a table—her characters may consider fundamental aspects of the nature of reality. They ask what is inescapably external, physical, perhaps lasting? Literally the clock ticks in regular measure, but time also stretches and contracts in accord with people's moods. The seemingly impervious natural world reflects human disturbances. As a person's mood changes, so does the external world; nature is even personified to have its "moods," as if storms were indications of emotional turbulence and clear skies of "Mother Nature's" happiness. In the largest cycles of cosmic time that exist beyond individual perception, a day matters very little, and a year is no more than a series of predictable events: sowing, reaping; the fertile spring and the autumn harvest. But to the individual, a year, even a day, may be eternal—or eternally significant. So then, Virginia Woolf asks, and her characters ask, what is external to people? What is "real"? To what finally does that oft-repeated term, "reality," refer: what the human perceives as significant or what is somehow (but then, how?) untouched by us?

The world which Virginia Woolf's men and women observe around them and in which they must struggle to survive is an ocean whose surface is as troubled as its depths are unknown. And this image stands for each of them as well. They are as unknown and unfathomable to themselves as to each other. Their lives are tangled in desires and needs and frustrations, lack of understanding, and a keen awareness of complexity, that unknown but fascinating "shadow" at the center of it all. How are they to live in such a world, how can they find meaning and value? The ultimate questions are these: what has significance, and how can anything in this unruly world have (or be given) meaning, stability, value, perhaps permanence? Knowledge, social order, love, friendship, art—these could possibly replace faith in God or church, the traditional rewards of the family, but only possibly. They are options to consider, according to both the novelist and her characters. Since Virginia Woolf is a novelist, not a philosopher whose developing ideas can be traced from book to book, the exploration is part of her characters as the mode of questioning is part of her art.

The obsessive questioning takes several forms. Questions are asked directly by the author or narrator and slightly less directly by the characters. Questions are also posed by stylistic means. Through the more difficult but more interesting means of language, structure, image, and symbol, Virginia Woolf can ask her questions and present the (temporary) crystallization of her ideas. There are three broad areas of experimentation, fitting the three major areas of concern: characterization, imagery, and structure. Woolf develops new modes of characterization and variations on traditional actions in response to the question of identity. New value systems make previously acceptable forms of behavior unacceptable, and thus she rejects a plot structure based on direct action. If simple chronology is neither accurate nor adequate, then a structure based on time is also inadequate and must be revised. If assertions are replaced by questions, then vagueness and distrust of absolutes evolve: the externally significant is replaced by the internally and only potentially significant; direct statement by image and symbol.

Characterization: the question of identity—If the boundaries of individual existence are not clear-cut in life, then they cannot be simply drawn in fiction. Virginia Woolf's solution is to allow character to melt into character, one identity dependent on another. If what goes on inside a person is of greatest importance, then, she suggests, that is what must be presented. It will be difficult to do so because she must try out new methods of presentation from which a lack of clarity may result. If individual identity is not the whole of human existence, if an individual is also symbolic, representative, a part of a larger human community, then the author must find a means of characterization to cope with this, presenting characters as both unique and typical.

Image and symbol—from relatively traditional beginnings,

Virginia Woolf gradually develops striking uses of image and symbol to represent her complex vision of man. Thus, for example, image-sharing becomes one technical means of displaying the relation between characters. In a logic analogous to Jung's idea of the existence of universally shared images (archetypes), Virginia Woolf selectively offers motifs which her characters share, nonverbally and indirectly. An idea, a picture, a feeling which one character reveals only in his thoughts and only to the reader suddenly is present in the mind of another character. A recurring motif may also be used to reveal the simultaneity of events or to suggest a symbolic link between two people. And in Virginia Woolf's fiction, images increasingly become symbols, with associations beyond the specific example and reference outside the specific work. The major series of symbols involves water, whether the waves, the sea, a lighthouse, or quiet tide-pools. The multi-leveled significance of such symbols is made apparent in the whole body of her work, in which the sea takes on a cluster of meanings—the traditional ones, like birth, death, flux, and eternity, and also new ones—the complexity of man, who is eternal and unchanging yet at the same time is as ephemeral in his individual identity as a single wave. (Symbol and image, clearly, become vehicles for characterization, and thus for the conceptions of human life which interest Virginia Woolf.)

Structure—if people are as complex as all of this implies, if simple chronology is not the only kind of time, if the traditional values do not apply, then the conventional ordering of action into plot is probably inappropriate. Marriage cannot provide a convenient conclusion to a novel if marriage is not seen as either an end to life or the only goal. The hero cannot be sent off to prove himself in war if war is not regarded as an opportunity to assert manhood or to support such conventional values as patriotism. Straight chronology is inadequate, so the novel of growth and development, even the assumption that such processes occur, likewise becomes inadequate, or at least inaccurate. Life just isn't "like this," so fiction cannot be. Thus Virginia Woolf and a few of her more adventurous contemporaries argue, and having argued this, they introduce new patterns to fiction.

I *Experiments in Form: Short Stories*

Virginia Woolf's interest in formal experimentation obviously affected the shape of all of her work. The first two novels, *The Voyage Out* and *Night and Day*, display the persistent questioning and the consistent themes, but only tentatively break free of traditional form. *Jacob's Room* is the first of the truly experimental novels and it, and *Mrs. Dalloway* which quickly followed it, deal more surely and overtly with the question of identity and the concomitant problems of characterization than the later novels. *To the Lighthouse* and *The Waves*, the major works of a period of intense activity, display an increasing interest in image and symbol: *The Waves* is partly a novel about characterization (it is also about other persistent concerns, especially the role and possibilities of art in the modern world), but even its method of characterization includes new uses of image and symbol. In her next-to-last novel, *The Years*, Virginia Woolf consciously returned to a traditional plot structure; in her last novel, *Between the Acts*, she completely destroys this mold, producing a book which (with the possible exception of *The Waves*) is more unusually patterned than any of her novels.

Throughout her career Virginia Woolf wrote short stories which were brief enough to sustain the flight of a new design and so offer an opportunity for experimentation.[1] Her stories deserve a more detailed study than is possible here.[2] She used this form in a variety of ways, producing tales with direct action and more or less traditional plot structure, character sketches, and impressionistic or symbolic pieces with little or no apparent action. People ride on trains or go to parties, marriages take place or collapse, pottery is broken and pictures fall from walls, crises occur and decisions are made or postponed. But these are external events; what matters is what happens inside the characters.

A description of a concert offers a chance to examine the wanderings of the listeners' minds, their imaginations and memories—a continuo constantly modulated and highlighted by reiterated motifs of casual chatter about the music, about the audience, about other events ("The String Quartet"). A woman arriving at a party unfashionably dressed goes through the outward motions of appropriate social behavior; inwardly she is tormented by this symbolic proof of her failure ("The New Dress"). In "An Unwritten Novel" the narrator observes a woman on a train and endows her with a name, a personality, and a story which seem to fit her appearance. The limit of perception is thus asserted when "Miss Minnie Marsh," unmarried and alone according to the imaginative narrator, is met at the station by her son. "The Mark on the Wall" also examines perception and creativity. The narrator glimpses a spot on the wall and in an apparently free but actually structured associational flow, imagines what it might be. The final identification of the mark as a snail is insignificant; what intrigues both author and reader is the variety of feelings and thoughts stimulated by the very vagueness of the observed item.

Not all of the stories are so overtly purposeful; few in fact make any such assertions of theme, even indirectly. Rather they are symbolic sketches, delicate evocations of the senses, acute insights into people's minds and hearts. "Kew Gardens" is especially notable for the variety and delicacy of its imagery: colors (yellow, pink, black, white, green-blue), textures (wax candles, square silver shoe buckles, drops of water), sights and sounds (butterflies, birds, airplanes, automobiles, voices). In "Lappin and Lapinova" occur a nearly traditional love story and a normal (though condensed) chronology. A recently married couple first enjoy creating a private world for themselves and then watch their closeness dissolve, evidenced by the destruction of that world. But it is the symbolism which makes the story work, even to the point of explaining the actual events. They are the only inhabitants of a dream world through which they express their solidarity in isolation against the "real" world, and they imagine themselves to be two rabbitlike creatures, King Lappin and Queen Lapinova. By means of symbols the story's conclusion tells of the failure of their love. When the woman says to her husband, " 'It's Lapinova . . . I've lost her!' " he answers with a frown and a grin, " 'Yes . . . Poor Lapinova.' " He straightens his tie and continues, " 'caught in a trap . . . killed.' " A half-sentence later the story concludes cryptically: "So that was the end of that marriage" (78).

Seeds of what later appears more fully and sometimes more experimentally developed in her longer fiction are present in Virginia Woolf's short stories. But her ability to probe with a degree of care impossible in a short story is one of the strengths which make the longer works more deserving of attention.

II   The Voyage Out

There are at least three "voyages" referred to in the title of Virginia Woolf's first novel, *The Voyage Out*. The heroine's literal voyage by ship makes possible the series of events which result in her two symbolic voyages: one, the maturation of a young woman out of childhood, and the other the movement out of life to death at the novel's end. The sea voyage is a familiar literary symbol for life:

the ship is a self-enclosed world, isolating its passengers in a microcosm of society, thereby intensifying the significance of all that happens to them. The motif occurs repeatedly in literature (for example in Forster's *Passage to India*, Conrad's *Lord Jim*, and Joyce's *Ulysses*). The two symbolic voyages incorporate the traditional structure of one kind of novel: the development of the central character (a *Bildungsroman*) and a conclusion as clear-cut as his or her death.

Rachel Vinrace, the heroine, is a talented amateur musician whose isolated if not deprived upbringing makes her seem considerably younger than her twenty-four years. Raised by two aunts after her mother's death, she meets few of her contemporaries and is left unaware of the questions which usually bother them. She has little formal education and neither interest nor grace in social encounters. Like her creator at her age, Rachel knows almost nothing about the relations between men and women, is innocent of love, and ignorant about sex. She too is involved in art (music) but even this is an interest which though intense is not exclusive. She is presented as playing the piano responsively as well as proficiently, a clue to her hidden capacity for feeling.

On board her father's ship Rachel is befriended by her aunt Helen, who at first finds Rachel uninteresting but in time recognizes Rachel's deprivation and her capacity for growth. Feeling that her niece must be given a chance to develop, Helen invites Rachel to join her and her husband, Ridley Ambrose, during their prolonged stay in an unspecified South American country. Rachel accepts, and the second part of the novel opens with the trio at the villa, still in a world isolated from English reality and even in some ways from English social norms.

Here what her aunt hoped for happens to Rachel. She is introduced to people more varied and more interesting than any she had known, she observes married life firsthand, and most importantly, she learns about love. She observes several potential models: a newly engaged couple; a frightened but outwardly brazen flirt; a possible prostitute who is evicted from the local hotel; several married couples who quarrel with, seem to love, or just tolerate each other. Finally love touches Rachel directly. This is the thematic center of the novel, an exploration of the Bloomsbury ideals of communication, friendship, and love.

Terence Hewet, the man who becomes Rachel's fiancé, is not much older but seems to be. He stresses his greater experience and

education, his consistent search for ideas compared to her compla-
cent acceptance of what she has been told. The development of
Rachel and Terence's relationship is shown in a series of events,
moments which have a largely internal significance. Seeing the
engaged couple embracing, Rachel is made uncomfortable; she
feels "sorry for them" (140). Besides revealing her truncated experience, this leads her to talk openly with Terence. Similar experiences allow Rachel and Terence to feel more quickly at "ease
than is usual" (157), and help Rachel to grow.

When Terence and Rachel admit their love to each other, the
declaration is filled with tension; only later does joy enter. As their
love grows so does their understanding of themselves and each
other. They work together, Terence jotting down bits of sentences
and reading novels, both processes he considers "essential" for the
writing of his novel called "Silence," about "'the things people
don't say'" (216) and Rachel playing the piano or answering letters,
or they walk or visit acquaintances at the hotel; but mostly they talk
together. They talk about their possible future together, wanting so
little, Rachel says, that the future seems assured. But of course they
really want a great deal: they want a love that lasts, and though
their youth makes them unaware of its importance, they want life.
They are still answering letters of congratulation on their engagement when Rachel becomes ill with a fever which leads quickly to
death. The novel ends soon after this. Two short chapters insist on
the life outside this small relationship: the hotel's inhabitants respond to Rachel's death with dismay, with the stock reactions about
the waste of someone dying so young, with blame and exoneration,
or with indifference—some cannot recall which young woman it is
who has died. Life in the hotel offers peace and the comfort of continuity, which is stressed by the passing of a natural storm: "The sky
was once more a deep and solemn blue, and the shape of the earth
was visible at the bottom of the air . . ." (374).

In this conclusion we see one of the novel's flaws as well as
Virginia Woolf's attempt to make her book more sensitive and more
responsive to her time than the available fiction: the symbolism is
obvious, the assertion of meaning is intrusive. The novel belongs to
genres which do not fit comfortably together. It is a realistic novel,
a comedy of manners with a strong line of development, and a symbolic novel with strong overtones of mysticism. These qualities
suggest the direction which Virginia Woolf's writing would later
take: the realistic novel was a form always available to her, an op-

tion she used two more times; but what interested her more was the possibility of escaping from that enclosing form, from the ordinary. These qualities (and their tendency to compete with each other) are clearly visible in her presentation of the main themes of the novel: communication, friendship, and love.

Terence and Rachel stand for anyone on the archetypal voyage of discovery which love can be, discovery of self and another. But they are not really typical; they are special, a fact Virginia Woolf acknowledges by contrasting them sharply with most of the other characters. They are unusually sensitive, cultured, and intelligent; they do not need to work for a living or to worry about money. Terence is introspective and Rachel becomes so; both are at least potential artists. In other words they are like the people with whom Virginia Woolf associated—the Bloomsbury Group—and like Virginia Woolf herself. Thus it is not just any friendship which is being explored. That they do not fully achieve the ideal probably confirms that they are fallible (which is to say human) and that the ideal *is* an ideal. That Rachel dies and thus the future of the relationship cannot be examined suits the Bloomsbury preference for the intense early exploration of love. It also indicates that at this point Virginia Woolf is not ready to take a close look at what can happen in the everyday experience of marriage. Finally, Rachel's death frees Woolf from having either to acquiesce in a sentimental depiction of sexual love or to deal with it directly.

When Helen Ambrose embarks on her program to educate her niece, she stresses the need for communication between the sexes. She writes about Rachel to a friend that " 'This girl, though twenty-four, had never heard that men desired women, and, until I explained it, did not know how children were born. Her ignorance upon other matters as important was complete.' " Helen considers such ignorance the result of a "foolish," even a "crimimal" upbringing. It is the source of much "suffering" for women and of many of their failings: " 'the wonder is they're no worse.' " Having enlightened Rachel, Helen can report that " 'though still a good deal prejudiced and liable to exaggerate, she is more or less a reasonable human being' " (96). It is up to Terence to continue Rachel's education. If he and Rachel do not achieve Helen's ideal of open communication, they come close to it. However, just as Virginia Woolf must in establishing the ideal, the characters battle against Victorian inhibitions in speech, in act, even in theory.

Like nineteenth-century characters, they agree that love is "enor-

mously important" (140). But to Rachel and Terence, love is important not because it leads to marriage, not because it involves social
institutions or changes in status, but because it affects the people
concerned in ways as intense and basic as anything can. It is these
interior effects which interest Virginia Woolf.

Terence Hewet first realizes he is falling in love with Rachel
when he finds he just wants "to go on talking" (184); he feels there
is always more to say. Whatever their subject appears to be—family, art, relationships between the sexes, the nature and growth of
love—they are really talking about themselves.[3] But for all their
openness, there are still limitations. They can never fully understand each other, because however unified they are, they are also
separate individuals, one a man and one a woman, one a writer and
one a musician, one educated at a university and one barely
educated. Their lack of understanding is revealed indirectly and
rather ironically in an overt consideration of that subject. Terence is
"puzzled" by "the simplicity and arrogance and hardness of her
youth, now concentrated into a single spark as it was by her love of
him," because their engagement does not affect him that way: "He
still wanted the things he had always wanted, and in particular he
wanted the companionship of other people more than ever
perhaps" (294). This might seem to reflect a difference between
men and women, or at least to suggest the relative multiplicity of
his interests and the wider experience of his life, but in fact it is
more likely just a mood. Later it is Terence who complains to
Rachel that " 'I don't satisfy you in the way you satisfy me . . .
There's something I can't get hold of in you. You don't want me as I
want you—you're always wanting something else.' " Restlessly
moving around the room, Rachel silently acknowledges the
rightness of his assertion: she "wanted many more things than the
love of one human being" (302). Their inability to see that ironically each has the same need for something beyond the other is
typical; the frustration this evokes suggests that Virginia Woolf
realizes the limits of the Bloomsbury ideal. "They were impotent;
they could never love each other sufficiently to overcome all these
barriers, and they could never be satisfied with less." Still they find,
in a moment of embrace, that their love enlarges them and makes
their world briefly stable, "solid and entire" (303). Limited as love
finally is (and we should recall that the Bloomsbury Group eventually turned to the greater permanence and significance of art,
even as a means of communication), it is tremendously important.

When Terence is with Rachel, he feels "he could not analyze her qualities, because he seemed to know them instinctively, but when he was away from her it sometimes seemed to him that he did not know her at all" (243). Instinctively, intuitively, even mystically they are drawn together, they understand each other and respond sympathetically; intellect, on the other hand, often lets them down. This separation of knowledge into two categories, roughly definable as tangible and mystical, or intellectual and emotional, is just one aspect of a cluster of such separations. Terence is acutely conscious of "two different layers" of "existence," one in which general talk occurs and a deeper one into which he and Rachel together can descend (274). Similarly, after her death, he is strangely satisfied because in some mystical world they have achieved a union which cannot be changed by time; but when he looks at a table with cups and plates he suddenly realizes "here was a world in which he would never see Rachel again" (354). There is then a suggestion that two worlds exist simultaneously: an everyday world of facts in which one can plan to marry, take sea voyages, live, and die, and an inner world in which those events have a different significance and even a different meaning.

These two kinds of life have their own realities; they can coexist for most people, and they can coexist in a single work of art. But to present them in balance and with grace requires a degree of artistry which at the time she wrote this novel Virginia Woolf did not have. *The Voyage Out* is too much a comedy of manners, too nearly a realistic novel with its lunches and donkey rides and dances, its mildly satiric studies of the perpetual flirt, the middle-aged woman, or the spinster who has devoted her life to literature as a profession (not a love), and so on, to support the symbolism which is thrust upon it at odd but important moments.

Let us consider in this regard two related scenes of major significance in the novel, those in which Terence and Rachel recognize their love. This is a crux for the young couple, who are moving from tentative sensations of something so vague that Rachel cannot identify it as love, so unusual to the more experienced Terence that he cannot decide how to act. It is also a crux for the novel which has been gradually opening out in scope, from Helen and Ridley walking alone like mythic figures on the shore before embarking on the ship, to the small ship itself, to the wider world of hotel and villa, and finally to the expedition away from that closed society upriver to a native village. Suddenly with this event the view narrows again: Rachel and Terence are alone in two consecutive walks in the forest by the river, and after this remain isolated by their love. The author notes, for example, that other characters live in a world of facts, "outside this little world of love and emotion" (304). (Later, after Rachel's death, the novel broadens again, first to show the people still at the hotel, and then to show the travellers returning to the still wider circle of their home life, England, and the everyday.) At this narrowest point, two-thirds of the way through the novel, attention contracts to Rachel and Terence. On the first walk, in an oddly tense and lowkeyed scene, they acknowledge their love. On the second walk Terence talks about himself, because he feels "they could not be united until she knew all about him" (281). This need to make oneself known is undoubtedly genuine but the conversation is too sketchy to make the emotion seem real. In truth they do not know each other, and there seems to be little joy of mutual discovery in their interchange. Virginia Woolf nicely expresses the doubts and exhilaration of the early stages of love and the relief from loneliness which affection offers. But the dialogue is stilted as well as abrupt, and the explanation that Terence and Rachel feel constrained by the near presence of others is not an adequate excuse for the author. The problem is that Virginia Woolf tries to use a method of suggestion to imply a continued and necessarily more intense communication. But because the book is more realistic than symbolic, we are unprepared for such indirection. This difficulty is lessened by the time-honored device of summary: "Now he would attempt again to tell her his faults, and why he loved her; and she would describe what she had felt at this time or at that time, and together they would interpret her feeling" (282 - 83). But the methods remain unbalanced.

The problem recurs in those passages dealing with the couple's physical relationship. That Virginia Woolf found it difficult to discuss sex is well known and of special interest to her biographers. About the later novels it can be argued that the physical aspects of life are largely refined out of conscious existence and are not of primary interest to the work. It can also be argued that the prevalent later modes of symbolism and suggestion make a direct presentation of sex less necessary. But here, again because this is so nearly a realistic novel, shrouding the physical in symbolic or mystical scenes is unsuitable.

That Virginia Woolf is aware of the importance of sex is clear.

Rachel, for example, affirms her growing sense of union with
Terence by an understated physical action: "A curious sense of
possession coming over her, it struck her that she might now touch
him; she put out her hand and lightly touched his cheek" (282).
What matters here is the feeling of intimacy leading to and secured
by her act rather than the contact itself. This scene, however, is
quickly followed by another, continuing the exploration of physical
love, but strange and strangely out of place in this novel. Apparently hugged or pushed by Helen, whom Terence has just told of the
engagement, Rachel rolls on the ground, aware of the grasses swirl-
ing around her. "She was speechless and almost without sense. At
last she lay still, all the grasses shaken round her and before her by
her panting." As she lies there exhausted after some unexplained
and nearly orgasmic ecstatic experience, Rachel sees "over her" the
faces of Terence and Helen. It is her aunt, not her fiancé, who has
touched her: like Woolf herself, Rachel seems at least as (if not
more) able to respond physically to a motherly woman than to a
virile man.[4] Rachel rolls in the grass alone, not in an ecstatic embrace (283 - 84). Overt depiction of sex is not necessary in fiction,
whatever Joyce or Lawrence and their followers may have tried to
make us believe, but consistency of method is, and it is lacking here.

If we must find fault with Virginia Woolf for inconsistency with
her new technique we must also give her credit for the attempt. The
novel points to the more successful experiments she would later un-
dertake: dramatic presentation of characters by observation of their
surroundings or actions—the contents of their rooms or the way
they place their boots for polishing; ever-increasing use of image
and symbol to enhance description or widen the frame of reference
beyond the individual; breaks with nineteenth-century plot structure through reliance on such symbols as the voyage or on myths
(Rachel, for example, can easily be seen as a Sleeping Beauty who is
awakened, if for only a brief time).

There is much in the novel to recommend it. The story line is
clear and interesting, the main characters carefully drawn, the
secondary characters presented with often biting (though never unsympathetic) wit. The main action is prepared for logically: when
some passengers leave the ship en route to South America the
nature of parting is examined; those left on board share a sense that
this trivial leave-taking is like death in its permanence, and that
each of them in time "would . . . be forgotten" (79). The struggle
of women for increased opportunity is remembered: Rachel feels

pain as well as amusement when told that too much piano playing
" 'will spoil your arms,' " making a woman unattractive and thus
unmarriageable (20); one reason she likes staying with the Am-
broses is that she is given "a room cut off from the rest of the house
. . . a fortress as well as a sanctuary" (123; cf. 154, 295). The sense
that man and his world are somehow united is frequently suggested,
so that, for example, Rachel's mind is "inextricably mixed in
dreamy confusion" and thus able "to enter into communion . . .
with the spirit of the whitish boards on deck [her father's ship], with
the spirit of the sea, with the spirit of Beethoven Op. III . . ." (37).
Delightful social commentary, a solid plot line, believable
characters who are also interesting all make *The Voyage Out* a good
novel. Charm, wit, and grace of language, those items that mark the
best of Virginia Woolf's work, make it a remarkable first novel. Experimentation in form, especially the frequent attempts to be what
Terence Hewet hoped to write, a novel about Silence, the things
people don't say, identify this as Virginia Woolf's own voyage out,
the first major work of an unusually talented modernist.

III   Night and Day

What was only a motif in *The Voyage Out*—the role of women in
a changing society—is in this second novel a central theme, Virginia
Woolf's first extensive consideration of a persistent interest. The
novel is a carefully choreographed dance of varying pairs, men and
women coming together, parting, and coming together again in
new patterns. The women are the beautiful Katharine Hilbery,
twenty-seven, of a family distinguished by its wealth, social status,
and especially its connection with a famous poet; Mary Datchet,
two years younger than Katharine, a country rector's daughter who
works not for a living but as a way of life; and Katharine's cousin
Cassandra Otway, the youngest and flightiest of the three. The men
are Ralph Denham, a lawyer from a middle-class background who
works for a living, not for pleasure, and whose interesting life is his
dream-life; and William Rodney, a poet of marginal talent but great
sensitivity and vanity. Additional characters, especially older
married women such as Katharine's mother, offer further answers to
the questions posed by the novelist: how is a woman to live? what
does marriage mean to a man or woman? what are the relative
merits of career and marriage for a woman? what is an appropriate
relationship between husband and wife, or an ideal relationship, or

a working one? These are the questions asked by heroines in
eighteenth- and nineteenth-century novels. They are also questions
of interest to other twentieth-century writers, from Forster and
Galsworthy to Shaw, but perhaps most notably D.H. Lawrence in
such novels as *The Rainbow, Women in Love,* and *Lady
Chatterley's Lover.* Woolf's characters talk less than Lawrence's
about their feelings and their philosophical struggles. But like
Lawrence's, Woolf's plots have symbolic purpose, even when they
seem most traditional. And, in *Night and Day,* as always, the
language and perceptions mark the novel as Virginia Woolf's.

Katharine, hesitating because she feels she is not in love, agrees
to marry William. Mary, although she loves Ralph, refuses his
proposal because she knows he loves Katharine. William finally understands what Katharine has tried to explain about love when he
begins to care for Cassandra. Katharine decides to help William
determine if he loves Cassandra and fosters opportunities for them
to be together, while she enjoys the beginnings of a friendship with
Ralph. As expected, the pairs are finally sorted out: William and
Cassandra will marry, as will Ralph and Katharine, and Mary
returns to a life of work and "causes." The similarity of the plot to
almost any of Shakespeare's romantic comedies is obvious, and it is
underscored by the constant references (especially by Mrs. Hilbery)
to Shakespeare—especially the poet of springtime, love, and youth.

Although the plot is simple and predictable and the novel is one
of Virginia Woolf's weakest, it is not trivial. Its exploration of
traditional patterns of marriage and new possiblities for the modern
woman fit it into the burgeoning concern for these issues in fiction
and in society late in the Victorian period and early in the twentieth
century. This exploration also makes it an interesting sequel to *The
Voyage Out.* Futhermore, the book is marked by Virginia Woolf's
wit, the charm of her descriptions, the grace of her language, and it
is peopled by unusually well-rounded characters whose believability
gives them significance.

Although each of the three young women chooses a different
mode of life based on different values, the novel makes no simple
assertion that one choice is best. Virginia Woolf recognizes that personality, family background and responsibilities, even the street one
is born on and the name one bears, all limit freedom of choice.
Nonetheless, within those limitations each character is offered
significant options and must make decisions which can rarely be
based only on reason. The intricacies of emotion are delicately por-

trayed here as being the cause of some problems (preventing rational analysis or behavior) and the solution to others. At first Katharine Hilbery seems to have no option but the Victorian one: to live with and for her family until marrying a man the family approves of, then to live with and for her husband and later her children, and so begin the cycle again. Katharine's family is as secure in its adherence to this formula as in its social status. Only Mrs. Hilbery's persistent romantic streak justifies her ultimate acceptance of her daughter's own romantic violation of the traditional. Although surrounded by elegance and luxury Katharine typifies one kind of late Victorian and early modern woman. Her mornings are spent on her mother's project, attempting to do adequate homage to the family's famous poet by writing his memoirs. Mrs. Hilbery is disinclined to work in an orderly fashion, so it is up to Katharine to straighten out the desk, the letters, the papers, and as much as possible, her mother's work habits. That Katharine would prefer to spend her time in other ways, such as indulging in her hidden interests in mathematics and astronomy, is not even considered by her parents. Nor is Katharine really resentful, though she is frustrated, for she is doing her duty. The rest of her day might be spent in errands for her mother, entertaining for the family, being present at family readings in the evening. Katharine, that is, "lived at home. She did it very well, too," and this makes her "a member of a very great profession which has, as yet, no title and very little recognition" (44). Living at home, with all that it entails in the sense that the Hilberys, their society, and Virginia Woolf use that term, had long been regarded as an appropriate activity for the unmarried woman. Describing it as a profession suggests Virginia Woolf's ironic recognition of the limits placed upon young women of her generation and also her sense of new possibilities, even (as she later argues in *Three Guineas*) that living at home might merit a salary. Katharine's role is supportive; her interests are suppressed. She hides her pleasure in working out intricate mathematical problems, because her family's interest is literature and because she feels science has an "unwomanly nature" (45 - 46).

Her engagement to William Rodney should be seen in this context. Katharine badly needs to escape from home, kind and loving as her parents are, and marriage seems the only chance: "It isn't possible at home." There is enough time, but "it's the atmosphere." She knows that a man too would not be happy if he "didn't do something" (194 - 95). But it soon becomes apparent that marrying a man as conventional as William would not offer an increase of freedom, change of responsibility, or different sense of herself. To her his demands seem exorbitant although she knows another woman might respond differently; she does not love him and she knows she is not what he really wants. Like everyone else (except ultimately Ralph) William sees Katharine as practical, reasonable, and responsible, all of which she is, but she has a romantic side he cannot see. Although she can consider marriage without love, she always knows intuitively that she cannot stand by such a decision.

Ralph Denham, whom Katharine finally selects, is a lawyer and a writer of scholarly essays but he is also a poet and a dreamer. He dreams of being a full-time writer, he dreams of a cottage where he could be free of the responsibility and the bustle of a home with cracked plaster and "six or seven" siblings (the casual accounting is his own). But mostly he dreams of Katharine, although not in the usual way. Before he meets Katharine, he is searching for a woman to inhabit his dream world. When he sees her he thinks, "she'll do . . . I'll take Katharine Hilbery" (24), meaning she will be that woman. But in his dreams he modifies her, altering her appearance slightly, her mind rather more, so that while intelligent and interesting in her own right, this ideal Katharine is also quick to recognize his superiority in nearly all things. If Ralph were to persist in his folly, he could no more have a satisfactory relationship with Katharine than William had. William learns too late that Katharine could not live for him or through him. He can guess that although she admires his poetry " 'that won't be enough for her' " (206), yet he cannot change his expectations. He even objects to her attempts to analyze their relationship, arguing in terms necessarily annoying to Katharine: " 'You were full of plans for our house—the chair-covers, don't you remember?—like any other woman who is about to be married.' " When she begins to "fret" about her feelings and his feelings, the result is " 'disastrous.' " He concludes, not very helpfully, that what Katharine needs is " 'some occupation to take you out of yourself when this morbid mood comes on' " (245). Katharine and Ralph, on the other hand, gradually learn to accept each other as real, even if this means that some illusions must be destroyed.

Their engagement is delayed by obstacles that were more severe at the time the novel depicts than they would be today. An engagement was binding, making William and Katharine's decision to dissolve theirs an action with social as well as personal consequences.

Moreover, because William can only further his relationship with Cassandra if she visits her cousin Katharine in London, Katharine and William agree to maintain a "nominal" engagement, pretending to be engaged while actually holding themselves free. It is during this time that the reorientation of the pairs occurs, so that the novel can end with the predictable double engagements. But the arrangement leads to family scandal which Woolf treats lightly. An irate aunt announcing that Cassandra has stolen William from Katharine and that Katharine herself has been seen alone with a man of a lower social order is mocked: "She beheld herself the champion of married love in its purity and supremacy; what her niece stood for she was quite unable to say, but she was filled with the gravest suspicions" (409). Katharine has conspired in the secret arrangement, of course, and worse (from her aunt's and her society's view) has considered living with Ralph without marriage. To Mrs. Hilbery the mere suggestion is " 'dreadfully ugly' " (483). But Mrs. Hilbery need not have worried; Katharine and Ralph even acquiesce to a traditional church ceremony although it is suggested that their marriage will not be traditional. Appropriately enough in a novel rejecting absolutes, Katharine notes that "much depended, as usual, upon the interpretation of the word love" (313). Still, Mrs. Hilbery had sensed that Katharine's engagement to William would " 'make no difference' " to the family, since even Katharine felt that she would care more for her parents than her future husband (143); Mr. Hilbery cannot feel that way about the engagement to Ralph, because "this man she loved" (499).

At least once Katharine considers remaining single, going away by herself, perhaps to study mathematics and astronomy (242). But she is not to be an independent woman dedicated to career or cause, any more than she is to be a submissive wife dedicated solely to her husband. To some extent, Mary Datchet represents the first of these options and Cassandra Otway the second.

Mary is neither a career woman nor a professional; she is not trained for a specific post and she works as a volunteer. But she knows what it means to work, and she learns that work can be a palliative to loneliness. Mary is presented nearly as sympathetically as Katharine, nominally the heroine. Obviously Virginia Woolf respects the dignified independence of women like Mary, though she may not fully understand them. Mary does not voluntarily choose to be single but devotes herself to work once she recognizes that her love for Ralph is not returned. She enjoys her freedom, especially having her own rooms, and she wants to work. But when she is most in love with Ralph, she finds it nearly impossible to concentrate on her job and must fight against her feeling that the "cause" matters less than Ralph. After her renunciation Mary involves herself in activity with a Society whose goals are carefully left unspecified, as if the cause itself does not matter. In making the best of what she has, Mary finds solace in having loved. As she says to Katharine, " 'one wouldn't *not* be in love' " (276). At this point, Katharine, still engaged to William, is well aware that she lacks what Mary has: her own feelings are "fictitious" by comparison (279). Later, Mary says to Ralph, " 'there's always work,' " and adds that Katharine " 'doesn't understand about work. She's never had to . . . it's the thing that saves one—I'm sure of that' " (391). Katharine has not learned what work means because she has always had something else in her life—not money but love, or the possibility of love. Mary conquers her despair and her sense of futility, and accepts her role as a "new woman," a working woman dedicated to causes rather than to a husband, spending her days in an office rather than a nursery. Her self-respect helps her to deal with her loss in a dignified manner. She is not defeated. But neither she nor Virginia Woolf wholeheartedly affirm the potential of her "chosen" life; both display mixed feelings. Mary believes "her future" had narrowed from "infinite promise" to "barrenness" (392), even though she would vehemently disagree with William's categoric assertion that all women should marry because without marriage, women are " 'only half-alive, using only half your faculties' " (66).[5] A job offers more than just a way to occupy one's time: as in Mary's case it can be a way to assert one's identity, to give life purpose.

Cassandra Otway finally opts for a reasonably traditional marriage to a man who expects his wife to share his interests, adhere to his beliefs, support him in everything he wants to do; but like Katharine and Mary, she is searching for a meaningful and satisfying way of life. Her search is less conscious, her actions more frenetic. Her family alternately laughs at her whims and despairs at her flightiness. Silkworms, the flute, poetry, and plays all interest Cassandra, and she turns from one to the next with youthful exuberance. She is more responsive than the others to new experiences. Even the Hilbery dinner table looks different when seen through Cassandra's impressionable eyes: "The pattern of the soup-plates, the stiff folds of the napkins, which rose by the side of each plate in the shape of arum lilies, the long sticks of bread tied with pink ribbon, the silver dishes and the sea-colored champagne glasses, with the flakes of gold concealed in their stems—all these details, together with a curiously pervasive smell of kid gloves, contributed to her exhilaration" (345). This is typical of Virginia Woolf's best use of her powers of selection and description. It is the first time in the novel that such a scene is presented in such detail. The very precision is evocative; textures, colors, shapes, odors allow the reader to see as Cassandra sees. The fact that such a description occurs at this particular time and not before shows how the author manipulates point-of-view: it is because Cassandra's perception is dominant that the dinner table takes on a new enchantment. The other characters, dulled by familiarity with their surroundings, do not see what she does; the unobtrusive shift in point-of-view, demonstrated by the sparkling description, subtly reveals Cassandra's nature.

Because Cassandra is so volatile it is easy for her to adapt to William's needs: if he likes poetry she can learn to like poetry; if he writes plays, she reads them with total approbation; if he suggests she study British history, she promptly takes a text from her uncle's library. Cassandra can thus make William happy by the most traditional means and simultaneously find her own happiness.

Cassandra and Katharine are described as symbolic opposites in several passages so direct as to be somewhat disruptive. "Where Katharine was simple, Cassandra was complex; where Katharine was solid and direct, Cassandra was vague and evasive. In short, they represented very well the manly and the womanly sides of the feminine nature" (341). Katharine lacks the "womanly" traits of coyness and vacillation as well as the softness which would allow her to mold herself to William's pattern. She is willing to run the risk of seeming unwomanly as she defies the traditional female role, whereas Cassandra accepts that role. Mary, who without rejecting the traditional role finds herself outside it, is never considered masculine. That Katharine's position may seem the most attractive is probably as much a function of the depth of her characterization as any intrinsic preference on the part of the author, and even Katharine's future is uncertain.

As a novel, *Night and Day* is raised above the level of just-another-love-story by its intricate structure and by its delicate and careful use of language and symbol. Although in many ways this novel was a step backward for Virginia Woolf—looser, more repetitious, less innovative, less gripping—it reveals development in its rhythms and tensions of dialogue and description. Consider, for example, this passage from a highly emotional scene in which Katharine tries to explain to William why she feels she cannot marry him:

She was completely taken aback by finding her arm suddenly dropped; then she saw his face most strangely contorted; was he laughing, it flashed across her? In another moment she saw that he was in tears. In her bewilderment at this apparition she stood aghast for a second. With a desperate sense that this horror must, at all costs, be stopped, she then put her arms about him, drew his head for a moment upon her shoulder, and led him on, murmuring words of consolation, until he heaved a great sigh. They held fast to each other; her tears, too, ran down her cheeks; and were both quite silent. Noticing the difficulty with which he walked, and feeling the same extreme lassitude in her own limbs, she proposed that they should rest for a moment where the bracken was brown and shriveled beneath an oak-tree. He assented. Once more he gave a great sigh, and wiped his eyes with a childlike unconsciousness, and began to speak without a trace of his previous anger. The idea came to her that they were like the children in the fairy tale who were lost in a wood, and with this in her mind she noticed the scattering of dead leaves all round them which had been blown by the wind into heaps, a foot or two deep, here and there. (243 - 44)

We can note four main features of this passage: the variation of sentence rhythms, the choice of words, and the uses of image and folklore. Early in the paragraph, when the tension of the two characters is greatest, long sentences are actually statements and questions joined by semicolons. Later, as the two are drained of emotion and filled with "lassitude," the exhaustion which they feel in their bodies is expressed in the use of complex rather than compound constructions. Adverbial clauses still create some long sentences, but they are no longer chopped into bits by semicolons. At his most exhausted, William is described in the shortest sentence: "He assented." There are appeals to sight, touch, feeling, and hearing, and images are conveyed by such words as "flashed," "shriveled," and "murmuring." Image becomes symbol in the dead leaves, the shriveled and brown foliage which reflects the dying of their relationship. Folklore too is introduced in the final image of the lost children, perhaps babes in the wood, or Hansel and Gretel. These features—careful use of language, subtle perception, implication through indirection, the development of meaning through style—are trademarks of Virginia Woolf's most important fiction.

CHAPTER 4

People and Characters

FOUR of the titles of Virginia Woolf's books are (or include) the names of people; one, of a dog: *Jacob's Room, Mrs. Dalloway, Orlando, Roger Fry,* and *Flush.* Each of the last three is subtitled "A Biography," but only *Roger Fry* can unhesitatingly be categorized as nonfiction. Although *Flush* deals with actual people and some verifiable occurences, the story of Elizabeth Barrett Browning's dog (even the story of Elizabeth and Robert Browning as seen by her dog) is hardly an ordinary biography. *Orlando* is also based on fact—the 350-year life of the title character scans part of the history of the Sackville-West family—but like its hero who is transformed into a heroine, the book is fact transformed to fantasy. *Jacob's Room* and *Mrs. Dalloway* are traditionally shelved with novels in libraries. Although Mrs. Dalloway has no direct prototype, Jacob Flanders is obviously modelled on Thoby Stephen, Virginia Woolf's brother who died in 1906. Jacob stands also for the youths whose lives were cut short by World War I, but there is much more realistic reflection of Thoby here than in *The Waves* where he is the model for Percival who functions almost exclusively as a symbol.

All five of these books are linked by a common interest in the problem of how to write about a person (living or dead, real or fictitious). The two novels, which were written first, most overtly express theories of characterization. The biography is not very successful, but that is primarily for personal reasons. The two mock-biographies are fantasies, never intended to be ranked as serious art comparable to the novels. That so many of Virginia Woolf's books should bear names in their titles confirms her interest in character and characterization, part of her quest to understand reality and give it form through literature.

What Virginia Woolf asks is simply stated if not answered: how can the new ideas about individuals best be presented in fiction? She struggles to do justice to her conception of a human being as in-

67

finitely complex, linked to ancestors, to contemporaries, and to the natural world. She is determined to avoid oversimplification while replacing the kind of characterization achieved by the "materialists." Some valuable aspects of the older types of characterization—the "acute sense" of physical reality, for instance—must be lost. But as the external details of "life, limb, and . . . property" are submerged, the internal details of character and a new sense of "life" are enhanced, and to Virginia Woolf, the gain outweighs the loss.[1]

While stressing what goes on inside the individual, struggling to describe characters as symbolic parts of a larger community, she does not totally discard external clues to character. But, in addition to the more traditional methods of dialogue, monologue, description, and action, Virginia Woolf uses motifs by means of which a character can identify himself or an acquaintance. Such motifs as objects, rooms, scenes, characteristic gestures, costumes, or thoughts are partly buried in the text, appearing and reappearing in slight variations, submerged in description or contained in the character's mind. In the earliest novel, this technique is embedded within a realistic structure and plot, and when employed, is handled with some clumsiness. Recognizing people in the appearance of their boots, one character bluntly says, "I always think that people are so like their boots," and as Rachel observes the contents of various rooms (a wardrobe, some photographs, an inkstand and pen) the author explains that "these small and worthless objects seemed to her to represent human lives" (*The Voyage Out*, 257 - 58). In later novels, the motifs may serve as reminders of the complex nature of human existence: some motifs are part of a unique past, a personal memory; others are shared, as created archetypes.

I   Jacob's Room

The identifying motif, this novel's primary innovation in technique, is put to special use in *Jacob's Room*. Virginia Woolf presents Jacob's growth from childhood through youthful maturity to death in war but replaces traditional methods of presentation with carefully manipulated "hints" of the sort described above. His life is conveyed by a scene on the beach in the morning or a glance at his cot at night. In Jacob's room, his letters and bills, some old shoes, and an armchair contain as much of Jacob as do the reported action and speech. Metaphorically standing with Bonamy (his friend) and Mrs.

Flanders (his mother) in Jacob's room after his death, we recognize him in the objects left behind; however, as much as we learned from the "hints," there is more we do not know. Like Jacob's friend, Clara, who runs out of room in her diary after attempting to describe him in twenty-six words, the novelist seems to leave the description incomplete.

The problem with summarizing the story of *Jacob's Room* is that to do so is to ignore its main point: that it is difficult, perhaps impossible, for one person to know another. To prove this, Virginia Woolf spends nearly 200 pages exploring one individual as if seen by observers distributed along a continuum, from his mother and his closest friends to the women he loves or is loved by, casual acquaintances, and an omniscient narrator. Jacob's view of himself gets surprisingly little space. Constantly the author reminds the reader of the barriers which make it impossible for one person accurately to interpret another's behavior, let alone his hidden needs or motives. To summarize, to label a person *this* or *that*, is necessarily to draw a partial picture and thus to falsify.

With this warning we can now attempt to summarize the novel's action. A series of vignettes pinpoint selected events in Jacob's life, beginning with a September day in infancy, as Jacob is playing with his brothers on the beach while his widowed mother writes letters. By the end of the second chapter it is 1906 and he is entering Cambridge University at about age nineteen (the age is revealed in Chapter Three).[2] On a trip to Cornwall with a friend, Timmy Durrant, Jacob meets Timmy's sister Clara. Although Jacob is involved in at least one affair and is attracted to other women (nearly all unmarriageable), he sometimes thinks of Clara. She, in turn, thinks more constantly of him, but social proprieties forbid her admitting her love, even to a friend or her mother. In his Cambridge room, Jacob reads poetry or his mail, writes an essay on Christopher Marlowe, talks with friends, engages in sex. He leaves his room to ride an omnibus, walk with one of his women, go to the Opera House or a party or the British Museum. A dip into the Bohemian life of the young artist in London and in Paris rouses Jacob to ask if this apparently free existence is more attractive than what its participants regard as his stuffy prospects—school and later office. However attracted he may temporarily be, Jacob goes on to Greece and will return to London.

In Italy and Greece, the pace of Jacob's maturation is accelerated: "he had grown to be a man" is the general assessment.

His chambermaid, his women, and "even" his mother "suspected
it," for his letters tell his mother (as she complains) " 'really nothing
that I want to know' " (139). In Greece he meets Sandra Wentworth
Williams, an older married woman, bored, sensitive, and obviously
available. She treats herself as part of a still life to be tastefully
"arranged" for Jacob's eyes, choosing her dress, her black hat, and
even her book (Balzac) to "suit the evening" (145). Jacob is interested in what Sandra can teach him about himself, and also in
the adventure. From Sandra, who wears short skirts with
"breeches" underneath (146), attention shifts abruptly to Clara in
London, whose "soul" is marked by "virginity" and whose existence is cramped into a white satin shoe (152).

Jacob is still in Greece when World War I erupts. As casually as a
series of gossipy comments about Jacob (" 'That young man, Jacob
Flanders,' they would say, 'so distinguished looking—and yet so
awkward' "; "His mother, they say, is somehow connected with the
Rocksbiers"), the first battleships are mentioned (155). The soldiers,
the heroes and victims of war, are as unreal as mechanical toys: a
dozen young men nonchalantly, "with composed faces," and "with
perfect mastery of machinery," descend into the sea to drown; on
land the army, "like blocks of tin soldiers . . . moves up the
hillside, stops, reels slightly this way and that, and falls flat, save
that, through fieldglasses, it can be seen that one or two pieces still
agitate up and down like fragments of a broken matchstick." On
Jacob's return, London is marked by war, so that descriptions of the
city and its inhabitants are in military terms. The next to last
chapter is a series of increasingly shorter vignettes about various
characters, finally returning to the main ones and always pushing
towards the conclusion. As the chapter ends, Jacob's mother hears a
sound which could be either guns or the sea; she thinks of her sons
who are soldiers but in her security worries also about the safety of
her chickens.

Even that small security is cruelly undercut by the final one-page
chapter, a picture of Jacob's room after Jacob's death. Bonamy
marvels that Jacob left everything exactly as it was, and wonders
what his friend expected: " 'Did he think he would come back?' "
Three sets of letters reflect three kinds of relationships in Jacob's
life: letters from Sandra, an invitation from Mrs. Durrant, and a formal invitation to a social event. The same words which had been
used to describe Jacob's room when he was first pictured there (38 -
39) are repeated, but now the emptiness echoes with a new per-

manence of loss: "Listless is the air in an empty room, just swelling the curtain; the flowers in the jar shift. One fibre in the wicker arm-chair creaks, though no-one sits there." The emptiness is in no way relieved by the presence of Jacob's friend or his mother, for they can only underscore a loss which for the reader is symbolic (the young soldier who expected to return from a war he could not understand has failed to return); but for them it is also personal. Mrs. Flanders's final, trivial question to Bonamy resonates with grief: " 'What am I to do with these,' " she asks, holding out a pair of Jacob's old shoes. Like his room, Jacob's shoes are something recognizable as not just *his* but symbolically and actually as *him*.

Left out of this summary is what should be at the center: Jacob Flanders. Jacob is first seen alone, standing on some rocks like an infant hero; the last picture shows his empty room, for he, no hero but an ordinary young man, has died in an extraordinary war. In between, many people try to know Jacob, but he is far more dif-ficult to net than the butterflies he chased as a boy. He is intelligent enough, an adequate student, affable, usually socially adept. The main impression the book leaves, however, is that his development was cut short; he is the archetypal "athlete dying young." Yet he is also, more (or other) than what he appears to be. Like any person, Jacob is too complicated to be captured by the nets of his friends or even the more sophisticated linguistic and literary traps of his creator. Virginia Woolf asserts this over and over again, sometimes in subtle or interesting ways and sometimes with irritating stridency or coyness.

When Jacob goes up to Cambridge for the first time, he rides in a railway carriage with a querulous woman, whose impressions provide an outsider's view of Jacob as well as an opportunity for the author to ride her hobbyhorse. To her Jacob appears so "powerfully built" as to be perhaps a threat; but "taking note of socks (loose), of tie (shabby)" and of his face ("firm, yet youthful, indifferent, un-conscious") she decides her fears are foolish. Virginia Woolf will simply not let the reader determine the accuracy of this assessment. Although she does not say what parts of the impression are correct, the author insists that "Nobody sees anyone as he is, let alone an elderly lady sitting opposite a strange young man in a railway carriage." Next follows an assertion frequently reiterated, that "it is no use trying to sum people up. One must follow hints . . ." (30 - 31; cf. 154).

As Virginia Woolf argues in such essays as "Modern Fiction" and

"Mr. Bennett and Mrs. Brown," life is not orderly and the reality of characters cannot therefore be measured in terms of the accuracy of costume and setting. She is willing to give "hints" of what is "said" and "done"; that is, of physical existence. What is "said" and "done" can be displayed in a traditional fashion; where Virginia Woolf first varies the vehicle of the realistic novel is in limiting herself to hints. But she further follows her own theoretical pronouncements in de-emphasizing what the "materialists" emphasize, the "unimportant" externals, instead seeking to uncover the essence of Jacob, her "Mrs. Brown."[3] Thus in addition to the narrator's direct presentation of conversation and action (what is said and done), she offers several other kinds of hints. Among these are Jacob's thoughts, which can either be a source of self-evaluation or simply more data for the reader to digest, and the thoughts of the people who have contact with Jacob. Such "hints" consume most of the book. At one point there is an especially interesting series of juxtapositions of the three sources of data (70 - 73).

Mrs. Durrant expresses an opinion repeated so frequently that it is probably to be considered accurate: that however awkward Jacob may be, he is "distinguished-looking." The narrator agrees that "seeing him for the first time that is no doubt the word for him," and offers a bit of what is said and done as proof—a picture of Jacob "lying back in his chair, taking his pipe from his mouth, and saying to Bonamy: 'About this opera now. . . .' " But the narrator stresses how little even this judgment discloses, since just looking at him would not reveal "which seat in the opera house was his, stalls, gallery, or dress circle," and whether his hands prove he is a painter or his lack of "self-consciousness" suggests he is not a writer. Even if "one word is sufficient" to capture an identity the narrator is not sure what that word may be. Other characters seem equally uncertain.

Clara cannot do justice to Jacob because she loves him but does not know him (and anyway her diary allots a limited number of lines per day). Just before one character's assessment of Jacob as " 'the silent young man,' " the scene ironically shifts to a picture of Jacob telling so indecent a story that he and his companions "shouted with laughter." A series of one-line estimates are probably as inaccurate as the assertion of his silence: that the housemaid was "very liberally rewarded," that "Mr. Sopwith's opinion was as sentimental as Clara's, though far more skilfully expressed," that his mother was "unreasonably irritated by Jacob's clumsiness in the house." Next comes an assertion that it is impossible to form a "profound, impartial, and absolutely just opinion" of any person. At one moment we have "a sudden vision that the young man in the chair is of all things in the world the most real, the most solid, the best known to us," but "the moment after we know nothing about him." That "young man in the chair" could well be Jacob, who now appears talking with Bonamy, crossing and uncrossing his legs, filling his pipe. Here is a rare study of Jacob's mind at work; usually his thoughts are intertwined with the words of the narrator.[4] Virginia Woolf successfully uses this opportunity to display the balance of public conversation and parenthetic private response (although presenting Jacob's thoughts as normal spoken English is less interesting than methods she develops later on):

("I'm twenty-two. It's nearly the end of October. Life is thoroughly pleasant, although unfortunately there are a great number of fools about. One must apply oneself to something or other—God knows what. Everything is really very jolly—except getting up in the morning and wearing a tail coat.")
"I say, Bonamy, what about Beethoven?"
("Bonamy is an amazing fellow. He knows practically everything—not more about English literature than I do—but then he's read all those Frenchmen.")
"I rather suspect you're talking rot, Bonamy. In spite of what you say, poor old Tennyson. . . ."
("The truth is one ought to have been taught French. . . .")

This offering of undiluted inner consciousness is useful not only in the facts revealed (that Jacob is twenty-two, that he enjoys his life yet feels he should settle down) but also in the tendencies Jacob might wish were not revealed (that he is noticeably self-centered, a bit aggressive, and loathe to show Bonamy his respect).

It may be that some things can be "conveyed to a second person" only by Jacob, and it may be, as the narrator asserts, that there is some element of "guess work." These are ideas Woolf elsewhere expresses theoretically, and here applies to the creation of both character and structure. But the narrator, like Woolf, is surely also right in concluding that the drive to understand another person is universal, that metaphorically we are impelled to hover "like the hawk moth, at the mouth of the cavern of mystery," even if to do so is to endow the person who is the source of that mystery with an enchantment and worth he does not have. If people were not interesting it seems novels would not be written or read.

Virginia Woolf offers glimpses into several characters besides

Jacob, in order to tantalize. At a party where Mrs. Durrant creates order in a way which prepares for such later social organizers as Mrs. Dalloway and Mrs. Ramsay, delicate hints of personalities are given. Miss Julia Eliot paints, the deaf Mr. Clutterbuck knows the names of some constellations, Elsbeth (who is not provided with a last name for three more chapters) loves Mrs. Durrant, and so on. Only fragments of conversations are given, often just fragments of sentences. Thus the author demonstrates both how people learn about others (through observation, conversation, "hints") and that their knowledge is always incomplete, though it may be adequate for coping with daily life.

Sometimes characters are presented in groups designed to suggest the wide variance of human nature or the similarities among individuals who seem very different. Using a technique later to be far more important in *Mrs. Dalloway*, Virginia Woolf juxtaposes sketches of several women, linking them together by event and time so that the comparisons are given force (167 - 75). First Clara, painfully aware of the absent Jacob, sees a riderless horse; next Julia Eliot notices the runaway. Julia, who comes from a "sporting family," is merely curious about this "slightly ridiculous" incident, whereas the frightened Clara trembles and nearly cries. Because she has an appointment Julia glances at her watch to learn that it is not quite five o'clock. Jacob's former lover, Florinda, looks dully, "like an animal," at a gilt clock striking five; pregnant and nervous, she laughs unhappily and thinks (though with another man) of Jacob.

The passage continues in this way for several more pages, skipping among a series of characters linked by an interest in Jacob, some thinking of him, some thought of by him. The next to last person actually to see Jacob is the village cleric, a former teacher who finds his student grown "so tall; so unconscious; such a fine young fellow" that he hestitates to stop him. He "let the moment pass, and lost the opportunity." Clara also sees Jacob, but when her mother looks out "she saw no one." These are the last glimpses of Jacob before his death, so the series of lost opportunities are doubly lost, and Mrs. Durrant's inability to see Jacob is an appropriate warning of his near-ghostly state.

Jacob's Room was generally well-received, though the author's friends were more enthusiastic than the reviews. As always the questions of quality and financial success led to different answers.[5] Her first full-length experiment in form, *Jacob's Room* was "a necessary step . . . in working free" (AWD, 51). It is understandable that we find imperfections, especially the author's insistence on her thesis and method. The reader may be annoyed at coyness like this: "The young men were now back in their rooms. Heaven knows what they were doing. . . . Were they reading? Certainly there was a sense of concentration in the air. Behind the grey walls sat so many young men, some undoubtedly reading, magazines, shilling shockers, no doubt" while "others read Keats" and "surely" one was "beginning at the beginning in order to understand the Holy Roman Empire" (42 - 43). But the same reader may be sympathetically aroused by the picture of Jacob's growing up and charmed by his typically human blend of contradictory and individualizing elements—curiosity, alertness, decency, assertiveness, indifference. Especially, the reader may be impressed by the author's increasing mastery of structural devices as well as her willingness to take risks.

II Mrs. Dalloway

As *Jacob's Room* is about beginnings, *Mrs. Dalloway* is about endings. The change results more from attitudes than ages: it is the contrast of England before and after the "Great War," the difference between looking forward to an apparently infinite future and looking back at abandoned or unsatisfactory goals. One of the two main characters in *Mrs. Dalloway* could almost be Jacob after the war: Septimus Warren Smith, who had been a soldier, is just about the age Jacob would have been had he lived. It takes longer but the war kills him too. The title character, Clarissa Dalloway, is in her fifties and the wife of a modestly successful politician, a Member of Parliament. Because she has been ill and fears death, Clarissa is especially aware of the past and of life's ending. The novel is the story of one unusually warm day in June, 1923, a day of ordinary activities (shopping, working, eating) and of the extraordinary. Clarissa, who is called the "perfect hostess," is giving a large party; Peter Walsh, an old and close friend, returns to England after five years in India; Sally Seton, another good friend from the past, unexpectedly appears at Clarissa's party. And Septimus Warren Smith kills himself.

The story is simple enough to be told quickly, but the structure is complex. Even before publishing *Jacob's Room* Virginia Woolf wanted to do a "study of insanity and suicide, the world seen by the sane and the insane side by side" (AWD, 51): clearly this is a subject which had personal relevance for her. Clarissa and Septimus reflect fundamental aspects of Virginia Woolf's own sexual and psychological disturbances. Yet, whatever Clarissa's neuroses, she is sane, whereas Septimus—however many justifications can be offered for his fears and his disgust—is insane. Such categories rightly make us uneasy, but Virginia Woolf offers adequate proof in the presentation of "the world" as seen by Septimus and by a whole series of those generally regarded as sane, and in a careful choreography which gradually increases the largely symbolic contacts between the two characters who represent polarities.

There are two groups of characters, one connected with Clarissa or with her social set, and one with Septimus. Clarissa and her husband form a nucleus introducing family and friends, politicians and socialites: their teen-aged daughter, Elizabeth, and her too-constant companion, the self-righteous Doris Kilman (whose name suggests an antipathy to life, not just to men); Lady Bruton, who invites Richard to lunch without Clarissa; Peter Walsh, who once loved Clarissa but now feels that although "the passions remain as strong as ever" a man of fifty-three "scarcely needed people any more" (119); and Sally Seton, who once ran through the halls naked but now is Lady Rosseter, living staidly in the country with her five sons. Among the guests at Clarissa's party is Sir William Bradshaw, a noted society psychologist. His patients' relatives revere Sir William but his patients fear his brusque rigidity: he "made England prosper, secluded her lunatics, forbade childbirth, penalised despair" until his patients share his sense of values: "his, if they were men, Lady Bradshaw's if they were women" (149 - 52). Her unsympathetic presentation of Bradshaw reveals Woolf's hostility towards his profession: like the patients she calls Bradshaw's "victims," she too had experienced useless "cures" and had been severely limited by her doctors (Woolf was denied the right to have children, forced to curtail her writing and to live outside her beloved London, and in other ways subjected to the indignities she describes through the character of Septimus). As Septimus's doctor, Sir William links the two groups, bringing news of Septimus's suicide to Clarissa's party. The figures who surround Septimus, with the exception of his young war bride, Lucrezia, function as types: a landlady, a few neighbors, an insensitive general practitioner, and the stuffy Sir William.

One way to explore "the world seen by the sane and the insane side by side" is to present two characters near the extremes of the

continuum of mental health and then make their worlds touch.
Virginia Woolf goes further, describing Clarissa and Septimus as
doubles, superficially different but with important similarities. She
uses three means gradually to disclose both their similarities and the
structural use of character doubling: a revelation of the natures of
the two, a comparison of their actions and situations, and a series of
formal links which bring them ever closer.

In presenting their interests, responses, behavior, and situations,
the author considers the two main figures and also their surroundings. She integrates this into the novel by letting Clarissa intuit
what the narrator of *Jacob's Room* insists upon: that "to know her,
or any one, one must seek out the people who completed them,
even the places." In this comment about the book's meaning and
explanation of its form (its reliance on memories and impressions),
there is an artistry lacking in *Jacob's Room*. Rather than by an intrusive author the assertion is made by a character (Peter Walsh
remembers Clarissa's saying something like this) and it is presented
as an older man's condescending if tender memory of the "heaps of
theories" which they, like all "young people," had. Peter
remembers Clarissa's explaining the "odd affinities" she had "with
people she had never spoken to, some woman in the street . . .
even trees, or barns." For Clarissa, this theory offers a kind of
secular solution to the problem of death: our apparent selves are
only fragments, "momentary" when compared with the "unseen
part" which completes our being, and which may survive, "attached" to another person or "haunting" a familiar place after
death (231, cf. 11 - 12). There is nothing startling in the idea that
knowledge of Clarissa comes from home and family, or from her
former lover. There is nothing unexpected about intersections
between Clarissa and Peter, Richard and Lady Bruton, Richard and
Clarissa. But two things are unusual: the meaning which is attached
to these intersections and the existence of oddly intense connections
between Clarissa and a man she never meets.

When Richard and Hugh Whitbread leave Lady Bruton's after
lunch, a "spider's thread" woven between the two men and their
hostess is gradually stretched "thinner and thinner" until finally, as
Lady Bruton drowses, the thread snaps. Shortly thereafter Richard's
drowsy thoughts attach to Clarissa, "as a single spider's thread after
wavering here and there attaches itself to the point of a leaf."
Perhaps because of jealousy (he has been thinking of Peter's
passionate love for Clarissa), Richard is suddenly "very eager, to

travel that spider's thread of attachment," to bring her flowers, even to tell her outright that he loves her (170 - 74). He does follow the thread and he does bring her flowers; he does not say he loves her though he believes "she understood without his speaking; his Clarissa" (179). The image of the spider's thread is repeated in the novel, along with other nonmetaphoric links, so that a picture develops of a vast network of threads running parallel or intersecting, occasionally tangled, occasionally snapped apart.

People are attached by threads to each other in the present, to their acquaintances and their former selves in the past. At the simplest level the novel insists that contact between people changes them. That is why, for example, Clarissa worries about Doris Kilman's influence on Elizabeth (will the thread between the two young women be pulled so tight that it weakens those which tie Elizabeth to her mother's world?). This also explains why Septimus's response to his best friend's death in the war is seen as abnormal: Septimus may initially have "congratulated himself" that "the War had taught him" not to care when Evans is killed but he knows one cannot live without feeling. Finally in his "panic" he asks Lucrezia to marry him; this proves no cure (130 - 31). A variation of this basic idea is the lasting significance of people who have shared one's past. Thus Peter Walsh and Sally Seton are part of Clarissa's present before they physically appear. It is not only that they have knowledge of each other from the past. Even now they experience a kind of nonverbal communication; as Peter says, "they went in and out of each other's minds without any effort" (94), an assertion which their knowledge of each other partly supports.

In fact, the boundaries between seemingly separate individuals are not always distinct even to the characters themselves.[6] Although Mrs. Dalloway never meets Septimus Warren Smith, in the recognition scene when she learns of his death she feels "somehow very like him" (280 - 83). Told of his suicide she intuitively knows the method used. Although he is a stranger his death affects her more deeply than any other situation, memory, or contact of the day. It forces her to think about dying. She may have "thrown a shilling" into a river, "never anything more. But he had flung it away." The Shakespearian line, "Fear no more the heat of the sun," which recurs in Clarissa's mind throughout the day, here becomes more than a mechanical link. Earlier the refrain is a device designed to connect Clarissa and Septimus, the young man who had once loved Shakespeare so much that he volunteered as a soldier "to save an

England which consisted almost entirely of Shakespeare's plays"
and the woman who introduced him to those plays (13υ). Alone
Clarissa watches a neighbor turn off the lights until the house is entirely dark. Darkness suggests its antithesis in those words about
light, and she realizes that she must go back to her guests. That is,
she chooses to turn from Septimus's world of darkness and death to
the daylight, the heat and sun. He has made it easier for her to face
life without fear, at least for a moment: "he made her feel the
beauty" and even the "fun" of life, that life is valuable.

Throughout the course of the day, Clarissa frequently thinks
about death; it is one of the obvious parallels between the two main
characters. Having a weak heart, she rests after lunch and she sleeps
alone. Her room is bare and her bed narrow, obviously suggesting a
coffin (45 - 46). Her bed is virginal too; the coldness predating her
illness is a lack of sexuality. Clarissa accepts as partly just Peter's ac-
cusation that she is "cold, heartless, a prude" (10; cf. 121 - 22). She
feels "like a nun" (42) in a room which is a cloister, grateful her
husband insists she sleep "undisturbed." As she lies in her bed she
thinks that she "lacked . . . something central" to most women;
her warmest memory is of another woman, Sally Seton. Their
relationship as girls was at most tangentially sexual, Clarissa being
much more aroused by Sally's daring and her beauty than by their
one kiss. Though Clarissa remembers best "the purity, the integrity,
of her feeling for Sally," "disinterested" and "protective," the imagery used is sexual and masculine. And even Clarissa sees the contrast between "such moments" and her present narrow bed with its
book and the candle by which she reads alone at night (46 - 52).

Septimus thinks about death even more than Clarissa does. He is
also like her in his caring about life and in his unusual sexual
responses. In some logic not wholly insane he kills himself because
of his respect for life: he rejects the strictures upon his life which the
doctors threaten and so, although "life was good" and "the sun
hot," although "he did not want to die," he nonetheless jumps from
the window. Yet just before this rationalization his mind has been
following its characteristically aberrant path: "how the dead sing
behind rhododendron bushes; odes to Time; conversations with
Shakespeare; Evans, Evans, Evans—his messages from the dead; do
not cut down trees; tell the Prime Minister . . ." (224 - 26).[7] This is
further evidence of the relative places of Clarissa and Septimus on
the continuum of the sane and insane. Clarissa is clearly much
closer than Septimus to what is considered the norm (that is, the

consensus or majority behavior). Both have experienced sudden and violent death. As Septimus's best friend was killed in the war, Clarissa's sister was killed in an accident that Peter thinks resulted from her father's "carelessness." Peter traces to this event Clarissa's occasional cynicism, her sense that "the Gods . . . never lost a chance of hurting, thwarting and spoiling human lives," and even sees her giving parties as a way to "decorate the dungeon" which is the modern world (117 - 19). She sees the same horrors as Septimus but unlike him has learned to cope with them. As Lucrezia thinks, "every one has friends who were killed in the War." In relating such loss to her situation, she evokes the majority which is the norm: "Every one gives up something when they marry." The difference, she feels, is that Septimus broods about "horrible things" (99), a theory very like the doctors'. Whereas Clarissa is at worst indifferent to sex, Septimus's inability to love is accompanied by profound disgust for everything physical. To him sex is "filth." Although he can talk about "Universal Love" he also feels that all literature (even Shakespeare) contains the message that "loathing, hatred, despair" characterize human relations (133 - 34; cf. 223 - 26).

Thus Septimus and Clarissa share like concerns (or obsessions) and their responses are not unlike, but the differences between them matter greatly. The two characters are doubles, the opposite sides of the same coin. In the earliest plans for the novel, Septimus did not exist and Clarissa was to kill herself, a plan soon altered. Clarissa thinks about death but avoids it by following her doctors' advice; Septimus kills himself, partly in reaction against his doctors' interference. Clarissa is female and a mother, Septimus male and childless (although they do share some sexual aberrations). Septimus is incapable of emotion (even his disgust is intellectual), while Clarissa, although accused of coldness, is overly quick to react emotionally and tends to exaggerate. It has been argued that "Septimus's character is in all essentials Clarissa's, but taken to a deadly extreme,"[8] and there is surely truth in this. Clarissa thinks of dying and Septimus commits suicide; she lacks passion, he feels nothing at all. In this can be seen a distinction between sanity and insanity. For example, according to Peter Walsh, Clarissa senses in the world a chaos and ugliness which she tries to act against. However slight her actions may be, they are reasonable. Peter can mock or "scold" her for being merely "the perfect hostess" (9), but she provides an orderly home for her husband and child, deals compassionately if patronizingly with her servants, creates physical beauty around her,

and gives her party guests a chance to feel secure.[9] In turn Septimus
sees an ever-changing world—now beautiful (a skywriter signals to
him of "their" plan which is always to give him beauty), now disgusting (when a dog, sniffing at his feet, starts to turn into a man,
he considers this a "horrible" vision of the future). His sense that he
has a mission is not reasonable: he is no more actually prepared to
tell Parliament that it is wrong to cut down trees (because they are
alive like people), that "there is no crime," or "there is a God" (35 -
36) than that body would be to listen. In the essentials, the world
which created Clarissa and Septimus is the same; in their reactions
and actions Virginia Woolf has indeed displayed the "world" as
seen by the sane and the insane.

Clarissa and Septimus never actually meet, and neither Septimus
nor Lucrezia is aware of Mrs. Dalloway's existence. Their union is
symbolic. A series of motifs serve as structural links: Clarissa and
Septimus (as well as other characters) walk in the same streets, see
the same official grey car, and notice a sky-writer. The insistent
striking of Big Ben and of lesser clocks not only serves as a structural
link and as a way to reveal the actual time of day or night, but also
is thematically significant for a group of people who feel that time is
running out.[10] Sometimes the threads are pulled tighter, as when
Peter Walsh sees Lucrezia and Septimus in the park and thinks that
Clarissa would speak to the couple (118). The closest contact is
achieved after one of them dies, when Sir William tells his hostess
of his patient's suicide. The sense of relationship which Clarissa
then feels with Septimus is either irrational or mystical, as they have
never met and they share almost nothing, at least in any ordinary
sense. It is probable that Clarissa is affected by the news of Septimus's death because it reminds her that she is potentially near
death. But the intensity of her feeling of oneness is greater than
that: she is also "like him," even if she could not really know him,
because they participate in a special way in the community of all
human beings, a community which exists vertically (through time)
as well as horizontally (at the same time). *Mrs. Dalloway* stresses
horizontal union; *Orlando*, the next work to be considered,
emphasizes continuity of time.

III   Orlando: *A Biography*

The vertical community appears repeatedly in Virginia Woolf's
novels. The idea is suggested by the structure of *The Years* which
traces a single family through five generations, by the allegorical

pageant in *Between the Acts,* and by several images in *The Waves;* in *Orlando* the presentation is so direct as to be fantastic. For all its whimsicality *Orlando* is "first cousin" to some of Virginia Woolf's more serious novels (AWD, 185). Its humorous nature makes possible an unusual forthrightness: what the other novels clothe in cautious metaphor, *Orlando* tosses forth with occassionally disconcerting directness. Is the individual a conglomeration of all his ancestors, physical and spiritual? All right, then, here's a character who *is* his ancestors and grows just twenty years older in nearly four centuries to prove it. Are the more sensitive people blends of men and women? If so, what better a hero or heroine than one who has been both? And, one suspects yet another question, listening to Virginia Woolf's imaginary dialogue with herself: do people say that my work is humorless or pretentious? I can play games, I have a sense of humor, I too can write popular literature. *Orlando* was very popular: in the first six months after publication over eight thousand copies were sold whereas *To The Lighthouse,* a far more important novel of about the same period, sold less than half that amount (3,873 copies) in its first year (Bell, II, 140).

Orlando is introduced as a sixteen-year-old boy in the Elizabethan age (approximately 1586), becomes a courtier to Queen Elizabeth, and is ambassador to Turkey about 100 years later when he is transformed into a woman at the age of thirty.[11] The next six years of Orlando's life include the prominence and decline of Swift, Pope, Addison, Johnson, and Boswell, and the entire Victorian Age, leading to the "present," 1928. In the final years, Orlando completes the poem she has been writing since the sixteenth century and gives birth to a son, thus ensuring the continuity of her family line. During these 400 years Orlando's appearance alters only to reflect periodic changes of costume and the character's change of sex. A beautiful youth whose "eyes like drenched violets" and "brow like the swelling of a marble dome" (15) are described in appropriately hyperbolic terms, Orlando is an equally beautiful woman. Literature, love, and the family home with its 365 rooms, its shops and stables, dominate Orlando's life. Before he is twenty-five, Orlando writes "some forty-seven plays, histories, romances, poems; some in prose, some in verse; some in French, some in Italian; all romantic, and all long" (77). Near the house stands a sprawling tree, the favorite retreat of the modern woman as it had been of the Elizabethan youth. This oak tree inspires the one poem which Orlando completes.

The hyperbolic description of Orlando is appropriate both because the book is a satire and because it is a lover's gift from Virginia Woolf to Vita Sackville-West. Vita is Orlando's direct model as well as the subject in the photographs accompanying several editions of the book. There are obvious parallels between Orlando and Vita, including details of the two lives, their attachment to their home, and their bisexuality. For several years, the love between Vita Sackville-West and Virginia Woolf appears to have been as significant to the latter as were her relationships with the two dominant people in her adult life, her husband and her sister. Whatever physical relationship there was between Virginia and Vita was fostered by Vita (an acknowledged lesbian) and in its incompleteness was frustrating to her. Virginia Woolf's sexual repression seems to have extended to women as well as to men, precluding a full and comfortable sexual relationship with any of her lovers, including both Leonard and Vita. Virginia Woolf's love for Vita Sackville-West may have found its fullest expression in the writing of *Orlando*.[12]

Two related themes give the fantasy unity and direction: that no one is simply one person and that time is not simply linear. In addition to "time on the clock" there are also both subjective or "mind" time and the cycles of years and seasons (what might be called cosmic or universal time). These familiar themes are part of the joke in *Orlando* but they are also structural necessities making possible Orlando's fantastic transformations and longevity.

No one is simply one person. When Orlando briefly attains the comfort of feeling herself "rightly or wrongly, a single self, a real self," she "fell silent. For it is probable that when people talk aloud, the selves (of which there may be more than two thousand) are conscious of disseverment, and are trying to communicate" (314). But a biography cannot present such a profusion of identities and so is "considered complete if it merely accounts for six or seven selves" (309; cf. 73). This *Orlando* does, by following one consistent character through the minor modifications caused by 400 years of life. Other characters in the novel are also multiselved. The Arehduchess Harriet Griselda turns out to be the Archduke Harry in disguise, and some of the same servants work for Orlando for centuries. Nick Greene, a poet and literary critic who is predictably never pleased with the writers of his own time, disparages his Elizabethan contemporaries Shakespeare and Marlowe and centuries later helps to publish Orlando's poem. No external changes of costume, status, or behavior can mask the essentially unchanging Nick Greene: pompous, greedy, always appealing to the glory of past writers (to Cicero in 1600, to Shakespeare, Pope, or Addison in 1900). Like Orlando, her husband Marmaduke Bonthrop Shelmerdine shares attributes of both sexes. Virginia Woolf uses these various opportunities to extol the androgynous mind or spirit, arguing its heightened sensitivity and creativity, as Eliot does through Tiresias in *The Waste Land*. When Shelmerdine and Orlando meet, each is "surprised" by the other's "sympathy" and astonished "that a woman can have a man's tolerance and a man a woman's mystery" (252 - 58). In each, however, one sex predominates: Shelmerdine goes to sea, a hero even when mocked, and Orlando stays in England, caring for the house and giving birth to a son.

Orlando's sexual transformation, her longevity, and her interest in literature all create possibilities for satire. When she is first dressed as a young English noblewoman, Orlando ponders Tiresias's question: whether man's or woman's is "the greater ecstasy?" At times she decides that the man's pursuit is "most delicious," at others, that the woman's being pursued, refusing, yielding is superior (155). Comparing her past and present costumes (dressed now in a hampering long skirt), Orlando learns that men have more freedom. Yet if a woman must be "modest . . . of her brains," she can also be "a little more vain . . . of her person" (187); she can cry, and she can "lean upon" another (245). As a writer Orlando strives for independence—and her style is individualized by a consistent romantic strain—but she cannot escape the influence of each period. In the late seventeenth century, as "the age of prose was congealing those warm fountains," Orlando's "floridity was chastened" (113), and in the nineteenth century, her pen produces only blots or "melliflouous fluencies about early death and corruption" (243). Marriage and the half-satiric setting of the Victorian Age allow Orlando to complete her prize-winning poem, which quickly sells out seven editions.

Orlando's longevity is explained by the theory of multi-faceted time. As time has a complex "effect upon the mind of man," so "the mind of man . . . works with equal strangeness" upon time. A single hour "may be stretched to fifty or a hundred times its clock length; on the other hand, an hour may be accurately represented on the timepiece of the mind by one second. This extraordinary discrepancy between time on the clock and time in the mind . . . deserves fuller investigation" (98). "Time on the clock" is the steady forward movement of chronological time, the measuring of a single hour through sixty minutes or a single day or night through twelve hours. The "clock" reflects, therefore, a limited portion of cosmic time, the endless patterns of days and tides and seasons. Time measured by the clock is like the "series of gig lamps" whose very order is found offensive in "Modern Fiction" (CE II, 106). The inclusive "halo" or "envelope" described in that essay is like cosmic time. The human mind or imagination can move freely in both kinds of time, manipulating chronological time and recognizing the individual's connection with the cycles of growth, decay, and potential rebirth which are possible in cosmic time and which are the stuff of myth.

"Fuller investigation" is accorded to the various kinds of time and their interplay in Virginia Woolf's fiction. Orlando lives simultaneously in specific periods of time, in cosmic time, and in the time of the mind. The novel is fantasy in part because it makes subjective time literal, so that Orlando ranges physically through the centuries. Constantly the author stresses the discrepancy between subjective and objective time, an idea reinforced in other of her novels. Orlando could "go out after breakfast a man of thirty and come home to dinner a man of fifty-five at least. Some weeks added a century to his age, others no more than three seconds at most" (99). In fact, very few people "live precisely the sixty-eight or seventy-two years allotted them on the tombstone." In the next line Virginia Woolf slyly mocks both the Victorian penchant for facts and perhaps also her father, a symbol of Victorianism and editor of the *Dictionary of National Biography:* "The true length of a person's life, whatever the *Dictionary of National Biography* may say, is always a matter of dispute." What most "disorders" the process of "time-keeping" is, the novelist gaily admits, "contact with any of the arts" (305 - 06).

In the survey of Orlando's four centuries, each major literary era or social period is briefly characterized with a jest or a biting thrust. The high spirited Elizabethan aristocrats ignore the suffering of the poor. Society in the days of Queen Anne is boring; the eighteenth-century wits prove to be fops. The introduction of the Victorian Age (225 - 30) can exemplify something of Virginia Woolf's writing in *Orlando*. One midnight at the turn of the century, Orlando watches as "a small cloud gathered behind the dome of St. Paul's." It "spread with extraordinary speed" until "the city was engulfed by it." Soon "a huge blackness sprawled over the whole of London.

With the twelfth stroke of midnight, the darkness was complete. . . . All was dark; all was doubt; all was confusion. The
Eighteenth century was over; the Nineteenth century had begun."
Next, "damp" creeps into every corner, insidiously rotting all
things. "Thus, stealthily, and imperceptibly, none marking the exact day or hour of the change, the constitution of England was
altered and nobody knew it. Everywhere the effects were felt." People felt "chilly," "rugs appeared, beards were grown . . . furniture
was muffled"; heavy clothes were adopted to conceal rather than
enhance the body. "Men felt the chill in their hearts; the damp in
their minds," and so "love, birth, and death were all swaddled in a
variety of fine phrases," forcing the sexes ever "further apart." In
literature "sentences swelled, adjectives multiplied, lyrics became
epics, and little trifles that had been essays a column long were now
encyclopaedias in ten or twenty volumes." This passage is typical of
Orlando's tone and style in its humor and wit, its satire, its persistent interest in literature and belief that literature embodies the
age, its careful use of parallelism, hyperbole, and periodic
sentences, its pointed use of imagery and occasionally inflated
language. *Orlando* is one of the light books Virginia Woolf wrote to
relax between the serious novels. Even without the evidence of the
diary it would be possible to imagine that writing this fantasy could
be fun: the author is less constrained. She can insert a reference to
herself and the present which would be jarring elsewhere. She can
even include hidden personal jokes. For example, Orlando is last
seen on October 11, 1928, the day the novel was published. According to Nigel Nicolson, the absurdly mystical conclusion in which
Orlando seems to evoke Shelmerdine, who drops out of a plane to
be with her as she waits at midnight by the Oak Tree, is actually a
picture of Vita by the same tree near her well-loved home,
"awaiting Virginia's arrival next day" (203).

Of Virginia Woolf's works intended for publication, only *Flush* is
so clearly a *jeu d'esprit* as *Orlando*. A recently-published play,
Freshwater: A Comedy, could also be said to fit the genre. It is a
farce loosely based on Virginia Woolf's famous great aunt, the Victorian photographer Julia Margaret Cameron, best known for her
photographic portraits. But the interest of *Freshwater* is more
biographical than literary, revealing as it does the kind of irreverent
humor Virginia Woolf loved and Bloomsbury delighted in; it was
Bloomsbury for whose pleasure the play was designed and whose
members produced it. *Flush* is a more substantial work than

Freshwater and a more public one than *Orlando*, but for both personal and literary reasons it is less interesting than that spirited and joyful fantasy of love.

IV   Flush: A *Biography*

Flush is Virginia Woolf's trifle; like the English dessert of the same name it is a delicate, tasty morsel, frothy rather than cloying, with little lasting power. The story of Robert and Elizabeth Barrett Browning is of course not trifling, but the story of their courtship as seen by Miss Barrett's dog is another matter. Everything is transformed by being mediated through Flush's sensibility, and what matters to a human and to a red cocker spaniel may be very different. The evidence in *A Writer's Diary* suggests that Virginia Woolf found writing *Flush* very difficult. She stressed the problem of technique, explaining that the subject was at once "too slight and too serious" for the treatment intended (185). Once she referred to it as "that silly book" (192), although she was not always so negative; she tended in any case to pair her books—one major, one minor or "silly."

When Robert Browning wrote in praise of Elizabeth Barrett's poetry on January 10, 1845, she was already a poet of some recognized importance. She was, however, an invalid, controlled by a domineering father, and certain that as she was already thirty-nine, she would never marry. After several months of regular correspondence she consented to meet her fellow poet, six years her junior. Browning's intensive courtship led to a proposal which Elizabeth Barrett at first rejected because of her age and apparent illness, and probably because of her father. Finally Robert Browning prevailed; they wed secretly on September 12, 1846, and one week later eloped (again because of her father's expected disapproval). Mrs. Browning's father never forgave her, but her health improved so that she and her husband were able to share some fifteen years of marriage before she died in 1861.

Virginia Woolf follows the basic story although she submerges most facts and does not hesitate to change others to suit specific needs. The demands of artistic unity lead her to reduce the three times Flush was stolen to one (113). Elizabeth Barrett's sense of her inferiority to Robert Browning may have induced Virginia Woolf to submerge Miss Barrett's achievements as a poet prior to their meeting. A reader limited to these data might assume that Miss

Barrett was one of those Victorian spinsters whose invalidism (real or hypochondriacal) led to purposeless scribbling, rather than a poet who was during her life more widely acclaimed than her husband (although the balance has subsequently shifted in his favor). As Virginia Woolf says in the book's Reference Notes, "it must be admitted that there are very few authorities for the foregoing biography" (109). She cites as sources or for future reference the letters of the Brownings and poems by Elizabeth Barrett about Flush; no biographies are listed though several had been published. She is less concerned with external than internal accuracy. After all, Flush could not be expected to know a date or recognize Browning's handwriting, and although the story is related by an omniscient narrator (sometimes permitting data to be included which Flush could not understand) usually the point of view is limited to his.

The specialized point of view is revealed by the book's opening not with a scene of Elizabeth Barrett in her lonely room before Flush is given to her, but with one of Flush in his early home—a workingman's cottage where he has the run of open fields and the company of dogs whose ancestry is insignificant. The mockery in the opening pages helps to set the lighthearted mood; at the same time it introduces one butt of the story's ironic commentary—the English sense of social stratification. Nobility in dogs is more easily established than in people, the narrator observes, for specifications have been set forth by the Kennel Club. Flush' smooth head, his dark nose, his prominent eyes, and his feathered feet prove to others as to Flush (once caught by self-consciousness) that he is "a dog of birth and breeding" (5 - 7, 21 - 22). Flush's first mistress, Miss Mitford, could have sold him for badly needed money but gives him in friendship to the isolated invalid, Miss Barrett.

Flush finds it difficult to adjust to life in London. The Barrett house exudes strange odors, his new mistress's room is oddly decorated with filigrees and darkened by curtains, and worst of all he is confined to that room, released from this bondage only to walk chained to a servant. He is torn between love of freedom and a growing devotion leading to love and identification with Elizabeth Barrett. His new loyalty wins, and Flush establishes himself in Miss Barrett's room as her closest companion and ally. As the years from 1842 to 1845 pass, Flush lives like his mistress in a "cushioned and firelit cave" (23). At least for Flush it is not an unpleasant captivity. Suddenly into his serene existence, and her truncated one, Robert Browning introduces something new. As Elizabeth Barrett learns to

love Browning she awaits his letters, rereads them eagerly, finds his
visits invigorating, and all the time grows away from Flush. She no
longer needs his caresses or his energetic reminders of the joy of living, and his response is acute. Whereas once he and Miss Barrett
had been together in a warm cave, "the cave was no longer firelit; it
was dark and damp; Miss Barrett was outside" (37). A year passes
during which Flush gradually accomodates to the intrusion when all
else (from sulkiness to direct assault) fails. Finally, he accepts
Robert Browning because he recognizes that his beloved mistress
and this strange man are somehow one, so that "if he bit Mr.
Browning he bit her too" (47). Such philosophizing is not strange to
Flush; as the narrator observes, his upbringing made him unusually
sensitive to human emotions (31 - 32). Flush becomes one of "three
conspirators in the most glorious of causes" (49), and though he is
unsure of the "cause" he is sure that some change is coming. Before
the planned change there is an unexpected one: Flush is stolen.
This episode provides opportunity first for some social commentary—that there is a vast gulf between rich and poor in Victorian
England, a fact the upper-class wants to ignore, and second for an
observation about Victorian social mores—that the unpleasant is
disguised so that the wealthy can feel free of responsibility. A writer
(Thomas Beames, cited again by Virginia Woolf in the
"Authorities") is taken to task for hiding in "evasions and
euphemisms" the facts about the living conditions, economic situation, and incidence of disease among the poor. The male members
of the Barrett family (and Browning too) are quick to warn
Elizabeth, frail woman that she is, not to meddle in such sordid affairs as retrieving Flush from the thieves (though the men do almost
nothing to rescue him). The elopement occurs shortly after Flush's
recovery. He is especially delighted with this because it is an
"escape" for him as well as his mistress from "this awful world of
dog-stealers and tyrants" (69). The greatest difference Flush discovers in Italy is that there appears to be no social hierarchy among
dogs: "Had the Kennel Club," he wonders, "no jurisdiction in
Italy?" As a "prince in exile" he enjoys both prestige and new
freedoms (75 - 76). Another difference between England and Italy
is symbolized by furnishings, something Flush can sense: the
"draped objects" and dark Indian shawls had been replaced by
"bright silk" and "thin white muslin" (81). The rest of the story un-
folds quickly. As the Brownings enjoy their freedom, as they write,
raise their son, and occasionally travel, Flush is with them, living to

be a partiarch who talks of life in London to Italian dogs and
ruminates on the eternal quality of love. To him love is something
"men can never know—love pure, love simple, love entire" (80); it
offers a link with the past of his race—Grand Dukes may come and
go, but the "spotted spaniel down the alley on the left—she goes on
for ever" (98).

When Flush dies the idea is reiterated that between all creatures,
and especially between some few, there are close, indefinable, even
unreasonable bonds. In this case, mistress and animal even look
alike. When Miss Barrett and Flush first meet and look at each
other, they have a surprising recognition scene. She has "heavy
curls" hanging on each side of her face; he, "heavy ears." Their
eyes are large and bright, their mouths wide. The "likeness between
them" leads each to feel: "Here am I . . . but how different!"

Broken asunder, yet made in the same mould, could it be that each completed what was dormant in the other? She might have been—all that; and
he—But no. Between them lay the widest gulf that can separate one being
from another. She spoke. He was dumb. She was woman; he was dog. Thus
closely united, thus immensely divided, they gazed at each other. (17; cf.
108)

In *The Symposium* Socrates postulates that people were originally egg-shaped, with four arms and four legs. "Broken asunder" by
the gods, the halves search through life for the appropriate mate;
rarely do the right halves match. Virginia Woolf generalizes from
this specific myth of love and sex to suggest that all people are part
of a universal whole though between some the links are especially
intense. But the echoes of the Socratic myth are quickly undercut in
Flush: she is human and a wordsmith, he a dog without the use of
language (cf. 24 - 26).

Other of Virginia Woolf's favorite motifs and topics occur here.
Sensory images recall Flush's ancestral past: when he runs or even
dreams of running free, the smell of hare or fox arouses in the dog
"a thousand instincts, releasing a million memories," so that he imagines what he as an individual never experienced, the "cry 'Span!
Span,' " the "crack" of ancient "whips" (10, cf. 25, 106). The subjective element of time, another repeated idea, is stressed. Flush's
initial "melancholy" after the intrusion of the Browning baby may
last two weeks in chronological time, but because for a dog "the
minutes swell into hours and the hours into days," his misery could

actually be said to have "lasted six full months by the human clock" (85).

Virginia Woolf's books reflect her keen awareness of her surroundings, an awareness magnified here because Flush's viewpoint and his tangible world predominate. Since "where Mrs. Browning saw, he smelt; where she wrote, he snuffled" (87), smell is the main sense appealed to. When Flush moves from country to city, from Elizabeth Barrett's room to a London street, or from England to Italy, he notices differences in odors, textures, and to a lesser extent, the sights around him: spilled wine, leather, garlic, incense in churches, a "tough relic of goat or macaroni" thrown from a window, the heat of the sun, the smoothness of marble, the "gritty and cobbled roughness" of streets—such, for example, is the Italy Flush knows (89). London has "swooning smells . . . the bitter smells that corrode iron railings; the fuming, heady smells that rise from basements"; the feel of "petticoats" as they "swished at his head" or the dangerous sensation of a "wheel [which] whipped an inch from his nose" (19 - 20).

By the time *Flush* was written, *To The Lighthouse* and *The Waves* had been published. In the latter book, Virginia Woolf pushes her experiments with point-of-view as far as she ever would. Thus the limitation here to Flush's point-of-view breaks no new ground. But it does present an often pleasant puzzle to the reader unfamiliar with the biographies of the main characters, because the reader's knowledge is limited by Flush's. For example, when Elizabeth Barrett receives a series of letters in 1845, Flush senses how important they are not by understanding the bits she reads out loud (for the reader's benefit) but by observing her nervous excitement. Only when Wilson announces "Mr. Browning" at Elizabeth Barrett's door is the hitherto unnamed correspondent identified for Flush and thus for the reader. The element of puzzle here is part of the fun for the untutored reader; for those familiar with the story of the two poets, the fun comes instead from being an insider who knows the secret codes and hidden meanings.

Combined with the sense impressions, the intrigue of plot, and the book's good spirits, this is surely one reason that *Flush* can give unalloyed pleasure as Virginia Woolf's more difficult books cannot. *Flush* is indeed a trifle, and its brevity is therefore appropriate: it is rich in sugar rather than protein, easily swallowed, to be savored simply as dessert.

V   Roger Fry: A Biography

Roger Fry was an artist and an art critic who helped to shape modern attitudes toward painting in England. He supported the avant-garde in art and he introduced the works of such innovators as Cézanne, Matisse, Gauguin, Van Gogh, and Picasso to an England generally unready for their introduction. One of Bloomsbury's most significant aestheticians, he had a notable influence on his friend and biographer, Virginia Woolf.

Roger Fry was born in 1866 into a family which combined Victorian rigidity with a strict Quaker tradition. Fry changed his plans of becoming a scientist when he found his interest shifting to the visual arts. He studied art at Cambridge and in London, Italy, and France. He became an art critic and lecturer out of necessity: his allowance was inadequate and his paintings provided neither recognition nor income. Partly because of inherent qualities (an independent mind and a native interest in art which his parents discouraged) and partly because of the influence of friends and teachers, he broke with his family's religion, values, and standards of behavior. He never separated himself from them, but there was constant tension over his studies, his lifestyle, and his marriage to a penniless fellow art student. Helen Coombe was as unconventional as he, but unfortunately she was also emotionally unstable. After a very brief period of "peace and satisfaction" (97) and a few more years of sporadic illness, Helen was permanently institutionalized. Virginia Woolf notes that before Helen's illness Fry "differed fundamentally from the man whom his friends knew later" (104). But this saddened man was not always alone: he had two children, his sisters and friends, and a series of love relationships culminating in what Virginia Woolf calls "a marriage without a formula" (255)—since his wife still lived—to Helen Anrep in 1926.

Most of his energies in the second half of his life were devoted to art. In order to survive he worked as an art critic: in order to lecture and write, he had to travel and photograph the paintings he would later discuss. He painted, because he felt himself to be above all a creative artist. His criticism was very successful, giving him much recognition, but his painting was far less so: he saw its limitations, and the critics and public did too.

It is as a critic that Roger Fry is remembered. He believed a critic had both responsibilities and possibilities, and he obeyed the first and exploited the second as far as he could. He felt that the critic must be educated in the traditions of art to have a sense of historical perspective, and at the same time the critic must study what is new in art to educate others about it. Fry's criticism is informed less by any set of theories than by his historical knowledge and practical understanding of the artist's media, challenges, and problems. Interested in form and technique, and handicapped by the lack of critical terms to discuss art, Fry designed a working vocabulary. But his major influence came through his active participation in developing modern art, supporting young artists, and introducing important painters to the public.

His unabashed preference for the work of the young, innovative artists led him into some misjudgments even as it enhanced his influence. To assist struggling artists, he founded workshops where they could earn a living through crafts while still having time to paint. During their six-year existence, the workshops may very well have helped to change the decorative arts in England: pillows, fabrics, pottery, and furnishings were designed, crafted, and painted. Many standard businesses commissioned designs, but others simply copied the original patterns or modified them to suit a somewhat less adventurous clientele. Finally the workshops cost Fry so much money that he had to close them.

Roger Fry is probably best known as director of the two Post Impressionist Exhibitions which officially introduced modern painting to England (see Chapter 1). Virginia Woolf writes that "it is difficult in 1939 . . . to realize what violent emotions those pictures excited less than thirty years ago" (153). It is only more difficult today. The artists whose work then created turmoil among the public and even the British art world are today among the acknowledged masters. The disturbing reaction suggested to Fry an essential lack of interest in art and a British "determination to harness all art to moral problems" (52); that is, to see art as representational rather than formal. But young artists endorsed Fry's judgments and their enthusiasm renewed his energies. The second Post Impressionist Exhibition provoked serious interest as well as more anger. Time has, as Virginia Woolf notes, "vindicated" Roger Fry (159). Fry also wanted to introduce art into daily life, to have the walls of railroad restaurants and school cafeterias covered with modern murals, and to publish an inexpensive illustrated newspaper about the interaction of art and literature (172). Most of his plans were failures. But he had done his work; he had sufficiently educated the public to prepare the way for a greater acceptance of modern art.

According to the *Biography's* "Foreword" written by Fry's sister, Margery, and ostensibly addressed to Virginia Woolf, after one of many discussions about "the methods of the arts . . . Roger suggested, half seriously, that you should put into practice your theories of the biographer's craft in a portrait of himself." But Virginia Woolf was probably the wrong person to attempt a formal biography of Roger Fry. She could bring the special knowledge of a friend and the sympathy of a fellow artist, but she lacked the distance, the freedom, and even the methods to write an objective study.

Virginia Woolf's "fact" books tend to be her weaker productions anyway, but Roger Fry was an especially difficult subject. She cared too much about him to maintain the impersonality for which she strives in the book, and she knew too little about the visual arts to deal adequately with his life's work.[13] When she ventures into art criticism her assertions are either hesitant or impressionistic; when she talks about his art criticism her background allows her to make well-reasoned statements only about his theories, not about his analytic observations. She is aware of this lack, apologetically reminding the reader that the book is not a study of Fry as an art critic (105). She appends a "technical appreciation" of Fry's painting "contributed by an artist" (299 - 301). But a 1000-word survey (itself less technical than impressionistic, and obedient to Virginia Woolf's interpretation of what motivated Fry) does not bring the book into balance. The family's interference created additional difficulties. Margery Fry and Helen Anrep asked her to write the biography but the Fry family retained a kind of editorial control.[14] Only because Helen Anrep insisted does the author deal honestly with Helen and Roger's affair; about her own sister's significance to Roger Fry as lover and friend, Virginia Woolf says almost nothing, and about other women she is decorous to the point of coyness. In this area, the prohibitions placed upon her probably supported existing inhibitions resulting from her morbid sensitivity about sex. The problem is that since her study is largely an interior view of a close friend, avoiding his love relations limits precisely the kind of material she could have dealt with so fruitfully.

What gives value to the biography is the sensitive probing which she does allow herself, fostered by her special sympathies with Fry and by the unusual access which she had to private letters, friends, and family. The biography can be mined for useful quotations (although the author neglects to identify many of her sources, they include letters from Fry to his family, wife, and various friends, fragments of his autobiography, and portions of his father's autobiography). Virginia Woolf's method involves continual interpretation of data; facts are submerged, allowing analysis and even speculation to occupy the surface. The analysis is sometimes Freudian: for example, she explains that "the shock" of one childhood experience, "still tingling" after fifty years, was sharpened because Fry's " 'first great disillusionment' was connected with his mother" (15 - 16). This also exemplifies her use of sources, for it draws from an autobiographical fragment psychological interpretation Fry himself probably could not see. Elsewhere the author indulges in direct speculation, suggesting for instance that when Fry was at Cambridge he "was overwhelmed by the multiplicity of new friends, new ideas, new sights," but that he would "perhaps" have considered the new sights the most important: his eyes, although always alert to beauty, "had opened fully at Cambridge to the astonishing loveliness of the visible world" (45). The inference is hers, and it is a convenient one for the biographer of a future artist to make; but is it accurate? Likewise, it is the author, not her subject, who judges the world to have "astonishing loveliness."

Two methods which she uses have special interest in view of her other investigations—literary and theoretical—into the art of biography. First, she attempts to suggest the multiple nature of her subject: like Orlando, he is a compilation of many selves, only a few of which can be dealt with by even the most comprehensive study. While describing Fry's life during the First World War, she uses the method developed earlier for *Jacob's Room*, replacing detailed analysis with quick glimpses at a variety of experiences—his personal and business lives, art, travel, even his domestic arrangments (frozen water pipes and the cost of coal). These are interspersed with comments about the progress of the war and how the whole nation was coping with it. She justifies this method by explaining that "these scattered and incongruous fragments" display how the war "broke into many of the lives that Roger Fry lived simultaneously" (213). In another section, to enhance the picture of Fry, she presents selections from his letters and essays on the kinds of things he would discuss at a social gathering: some of his ideas about topics as disparate as science, religion, and the arts are thus introduced very nearly in his own voice.

In the essay "The Art of Biography," Virginia Woolf stresses the need (as well as the difficulties) for the biographer to make his sub-

ject "solid, real, palpable" (CE IV, 221 - 28). The biographer is
limited because he must stick to the facts and may be further bound
to the interpretations accepted by the subject's family. The
biographer should have access to all of the facts and be free to select
among them in order to create a biography which goes beyond accuracy to achieve a truth. Or, as she says in another essay ("The
New Biography," CE IV, 229 - 35), "facts must be manipulated" so
that the "light of personality may shine through." The "inner life of
thought and emotion," she believes, should interest both
biographer and reader. She feels that such a biography requires a
method that perhaps has not yet been discovered. It can safely be
argued that in *Roger Fry* she has not achieved what she sets forth as
the ideal; no more than in *Orlando* has she successfully
revolutionized biography as she wished.[15] Facts were not freely hers
to use, and she could not bring herself to use even all of those which
she had. The unbalance in her study is not redressed by the quick
survey of "a number of unflattering portraits" of Fry just before the
book's end, passed off with the comment that "truth seems to com-
pel the admission" that in his friends he "created the warmest feeling
of affection and admiration" (290 - 91). The prejudice does not
make Roger Fry seem unreal; instead the reader senses the close
bond between subject and author. The strength of the biography
lies in Virginia Woolf's ability to give life to some aspects of Roger
Fry. Like Jacob and Mrs. Dalloway, and even like Orlando, Roger
Fry is a complex, multi-selved figure. If Virginia Woolf is less
successful in achieving grace and balance here than in her novels,
the restrictions placed upon her and the fact that the medium was
uncongenial to her go a long way to explain the partial failure.
However much a portrayer of character she may be, her usual
characters are imaginary, her usual touchstones are her personal
values and her sense of what is true, her usual medium is fiction.

CHAPTER 5

Image and Symbol

THE reader of a novel by Virginia Woolf is invited to listen to the sounds of the city at night, the birds in a garden in the morning, and the pounding of the waves on a shore. He or she is offered the flowers and mud of a park in springtime to smell, a rough stalk or the flutter of silk to touch, and wine, veal, fish, or the rich herbs and sauces of a delicate *Boeuf en daube* to taste. But most of all, the reader is asked to use his eyes, to respond visually to the world: a scrawny cat, a chimney clogged with soot, a willow tree by the water, a dress colored with the reds and yellows of a fire. The object most often presented to view is water—puddles, rivers, tidepools, and especially the sea. Although it has been said that Virginia Woolf pays insufficient attention to the physical (preferring to describe the inner life of feeling and thought), her novels are enriched by numerous appeals to the senses. Her imagery rarely serves just to decorate. Simple similes of course appear; in *The Waves*, for instance, Bernard emphasizes the crude heartiness of the school's headmaster by describing his "nose like a mountain at sunset" (196) and his way of "lurching into chapel, as if he trod a battleship in a gale of wind" (344). But usually the most direct image takes on added meaning. A color may identify or characterize a man or woman, as green surrounds the earth mother, Susan, or firelight the quick and lively Jinny, in *The Waves*. A young boy sitting near his mother expresses his Oedipal hatred of his father by a wish to kill him ("lean as a knife") with an ax or poker (*To the Lighthouse*, 10). Swallows which return each year to a barn in *Between the Acts* are one suggestion of the continuity of life through the centuries. The very titles of Virginia Woolf's novels are usually symbolic.

Multiple implications are suggested by the clustering of images or by context, but the most interesting symbols, including the Lighthouse, the trip to the Lighthouse, and Lily Briscoe's painting

97

in *To the Lighthouse,* and the many variations of water and related objects (beach, reeds, tides, whirlpool, battered boats) in *The Waves,* offer many possibilities which need not be mutually exclusive. Virginia Woolf suggests that this accords with her intention when she writes about *The Waves* that "what interests me . . . was the freedom and boldness with which my imagination picked up, used and tossed aside all the images, symbols which I had prepared. I am sure that this is the right way of using them . . . simply as images, never making them work out; only suggest" (AWD, 165). A character who represents many of Woolf's views explains this further, significantly by using an image. Conjuring up "a waste of water" in which "a fin turns," Bernard notes that "This bare visual impression is unattached to any line of reason, it springs up as one might see the fin of a porpoise on the horizon. Visual impressions often communicate thus briefly statements that we shall in time to come uncover and coax into words" (*The Waves,* 307). So in the novels we are given a sense impression and as the image reappears, often modified, we gradually begin to see a pattern of reference, then some significance which we may not ever be able to explain completely. Sometimes Virginia Woolf makes one or more symbolic meanings overt, through a character as intermediary or even through the narrator. But more often it is left to the reader to "uncover and coax into words" what the image suggests.

Light and dark, colors, flowers, ghosts of dead men, the communion of a ritually shared meal are some of the many images Virginia Woolf uses which have associations in other contexts. Because of the widespread knowledge of the Christian ceremony of the Eucharist, for example, she can present in *To the Lighthouse* or *The Waves* dinner parties at which candles are lit or bread and wine served, and the participants brought closely together, and expect us to sense that the communication which takes place is special. The sea is a reservoir of images, referring to birth or death, change or cyclic constancy, the human unconscious, the imagination, and so on. In fact, in Virginia Woolf's novels it can serve all of these functions, and more. In the individual wave which breaks just once on the shore, the sea suggests the fragility of human life; but as each wave is part of the whole pattern of the tides, the sea can also stand for the eternal in human life. The ocean can be productive, carrying Rachel on her "voyage out," or it can be destructive, claiming Jacob's copy of Shakespeare (*Jacob's Room*), drowning sailors in a storm (*To the Lighthouse*), or leaving boats wrecked on the shore (*The Waves*).

While a variety of biographical and psychological reasons could be suggested, it is also true that Virginia Woolf may have been attracted to the sea as symbol precisely because the traditional associations and ambiguous nature of the sea offer a wide variety of possible meanings. Images are not mathematical formulas and cannot be exactly denotative; what they "suggest," however, is plentiful.

I   To the Lighthouse

To the Lighthouse is like a two-act play with an entr'acte, each "act" (or section) dominated by the symbol which is its title. "The Window," the first and longest section, is set early one September afternoon and evening at the summer home of the Ramsay family in the Hebrides, off the Scottish coast. The cast includes Mr. and Mrs. Ramsay, their eight children, a half dozen friends, and a few others—a cook, a maid, some villagers. Through the first half of this section a drawing-room window provides a two-way frame. Inside the house Mrs. Ramsay reads to James, her youngest son, or helps him find pictures to cut out, while her mind roams through memories and considers problems of interest to her or her family. Occasionally her attention is drawn outside, and she looks through the window at her husband pacing the porch or at Lily Briscoe painting on the lawn. Her husband often looks at her or stops to talk, and Lily, an artist in her early thirties, regards the picture of mother and son framed by the window as part of the composition of her painting. The effect is partly ironic, because for all her beauty Mrs. Ramsay is not simply frozen as an object of art, and for all her veneration Lily plans to incorporate Mrs. Ramsay into the painting only as a triangular shadow. Other characters are introduced as they are remembered by or come into contact with one of these three: William Bankes, the scientist who fusses about properly cooked vegetables; Charles Tansley, a young scholar whose praise comforts Mr. Ramsay but whose insecure aggressiveness annoys the rest of the family; Augustus Carmichael, a poet of no reputation whose beard is stained by opium; Paul Rayley and Minta Doyle, who fulfill Mrs. Ramsay's unspoken but obvious wishes by becoming engaged; and the children, from the beautiful Prue and the mathematically gifted Andrew to James and Cam, at six and seven still too young to join the family at dinner. Nothing out of the ordinary happens on this particular day. Mr. Ramsay angers James by

interrupting and by predicting that bad weather will preclude a trip
to the Lighthouse next day; Lily works at her painting; Nancy and
Andrew are startled on a walk with Paul and Minta by seeing the
newly engaged pair embrace; Mrs. Ramsay presides over dinner for
the large gathering, helps to allay her husband's fears that his fame
as a writer of philosophy will not last, but cannot tell him that she
loves him.

As "Time Passes" (the entr'acte) begins, the lights are extinguish-
ed and the cast of characters prepare for sleep. As it ends, some of
the same people repeat this action: Mr. Carmichael stays up latest,
reading Virgil. When the curtain rises on "The Lighthouse," the
last "act," Lily is at breakfast planning to complete her painting,
and James, Cam, and Mr. Ramsay are preparing to sail to the
Lighthouse. However, it is ten years later. A decade has passed in
the brief, lyrical interlude which occupies less than one-tenth of the
novel, just about thirty pages. One night can blur into ten years
because without human intervention or measurement, the division
of a day into hours or a year into months has no purpose. During the
years of the Ramsays' absence "time" merely "passes," as the title
asserts. But in this period Mrs. Ramsay dies, Prue marries and dies
in childbirth, Andrew is killed in the First World War, and Mr. Carmichael achieves the fame which Mr. Ramsay so desires. In an ordinary novel, such events would be emphasized but here they are
deliberately underplayed, presented in stark factual reports,
bracketed off from the poetic description of the uninterrupted
passage of days and seasons. The physical intervention of two
women who prepare the house for the Ramsays' return can rescue
the house from "the sands of oblivion," "the pool of Time" (209)
into which it was sinking. The house is rescued and most of the people return, some to complete projects begun in the first act. "The
Lighthouse" section is dominated by Mr. Ramsay's determined
pilgrimage to that symbol of the past, as James and Cam are
dominated by their father and forced against their wills to participate in his ritual of remembrance. In scenes which alternate with
those of the trip, Lily also pays homage to her memory of Mrs.
Ramsay, finally completing the painting which depends upon her
vision of the older woman. James and Cam's hatred of their father
gives way to love as their boat nears the Lighthouse. "He has
landed," Lily says as she stands by her easel looking toward the
Lighthouse she can barely see in the distance; "It is finished," she
adds (309), in reference to both the symbolic journey and her painting.

Both Mr. Ramsay's journey and Lily's painting are memorials to Mrs. Ramsay, perhaps for her husband because he had quarrelled with her over the trip ten years earlier. It is tempting to fall into the trap of regarding Mrs. Ramsay exclusively as a symbol; she is the center of the novel and one of its sources of unity. To Lily and William, she is the archetypal wife and mother (a symbol of marriage, with her husband; of motherhood, with James).[1] She has been defined by critics as Eve, the Virgin Mary, Christ, and the female goddesses of ancient myths of regeneration.[2] But however greatly she partakes of such roles, she is unique: a beautiful woman with a capacity for social ordering and a penchant for meddling in others' relationships, who likes to carry her own basket when she walks. As Lily says, to understand Mrs. Ramsay one would need "fifty pairs of eyes" and even then the picture would be incomplete (294). *To the Lighthouse* provides a reasonable approximation of those "fifty pairs of eyes." Mrs. Ramsay is presented as she appears to her children and husband, to Lily, William Bankes, Paul and Minta, Charles Tansley, and at least indirectly to Mr. Carmichael. Even after her death Mrs. Ramsay is present in memory, especially in Lily's thoughts. Earlier she reveals her sense of herself through words and thoughts: "The Window" is dominated by her point of view. The omniscient narrator comments on her attitudes and tone of voice (for example, she speaks "compassionately" to James [26], or is heard "laughing" at Jasper, who "shared his mother's vice" and "exaggerated" [120]) and observes physical actions (Mrs. Ramsay shakes and twists the reddish-brown stocking she is knitting and measures it against her son's leg; she serves soup and meat at dinner, strides purposefully across the lawn, etc.). Finally, the narrator introduces the perspective of society to the various eyes regarding Mrs. Ramsay, quoting an unidentified "they" or "people": for example, "was it nothing but looks, people said" (46). With the partial exceptions of Lily and Mr. Ramsay, other characters exist mainly to enhance knowledge of the one central figure. The relationship between Paul and Minta, for instance, matters primarily because it is fostered by Mrs. Ramsay and it reflects in its foundation and its failure upon her desire for social ordering.

Mrs. Ramsay is a complex individual, one of Virginia Woolf's most fully developed characters. She sometimes seems a goddess of fertility and regeneration, with her eight children and her insistence that "all must marry" (77), that marriage is always "an admirable idea" (109). Her essentially anti-intellectual approach encourages this sense: it is not that she lacks intelligence but that she "thinks" emotionally, considering feelings more important than facts. She seems honestly to believe what she says to Lily—that "an un- married woman has missed the best of life" (77). Yet she knows that marriage involves worrying about greenhouse bills and protecting her husband from such worry, and that traditional sex roles may not be satisfactory.

In a passage whose significance is carried as much by imagery as by action, Mrs. Ramsay offers comfort to her husband—the sym- pathetic encouragement which is traditionally the woman's to give—in overtly masculine terms (51 - 63). Mr. Ramsay has been thinking of the difficulty of his work and the probable brevity of his fame, while the narrator provides good-humored mockery, com- paring his situation to that of such classic heroes as the captain of a ship "exposed on a broiling sea with six biscuits and a flask of water" or the leader of a "desolate expedition across the icy solitudes of the Polar region." Such a hero cannot be blamed, we are told, if at times he needs his greatness confirmed, as Mr. Ram- say now approaches his wife "demanding sympathy." She "braced herself, and, half turning, seemed to raise herself with an effort, and at once to pour erect into the air a rain of energy, a column of spray, looking at the same time animated and alive as if all her energies were being fused into force . . . and into this delicious fecundity, this fountain and spray of life, the fatal sterility of the male plunged itself, like a beak of brass, barren and bare." The images shift between male and female, but it is the woman who possesses the energy and power described as phallic. She is able to solace him, so that (in a final, maternal image) he is "filled with her words, like a child who drops off satisfied . . . restored, renewed." But the effort exhausts her; although "there throbbed through her . . . the rap- ture of successful creation," she is physically exhausted. What she feels is not the comfortable exhaustion which follows a sexual en- counter (as this symbolically is) but something "faintly dis- agreeable," a "dissatisfaction" with being forced to feel "finer than her husband." Believing he is "infinitely the more important" of the two, she dislikes his coming to her overtly for help, thus letting others see his dependence. She is also disturbed that she cannot tell him "the truth," cannot rely on him for help with the greenhouse bill or tell him that "his last book was not quite his best book." She is reminded, simply, "of the inadequacy of human relationships, that the most perfect was flawed." But she is not perfect: an earth mother whose very generosity is suspect (she feels that "this desire of hers to give, to help, was vanity" [65]), and who wears a "deerstalker's hat" (47) when striding after the children who are elsewhere described as "stags" (16). Her knowledge is intuitive, but she can be contemplative although she tries to hide this from others (104). Like Mrs. Dalloway, she is a social organizer, and like that earlier character, she intends her parties to be gifts. She arranges the guests, candles, and food as Lily prepares her paints and canvas, and for much the same reason: each is striving to impose order on the chaos of daily life, to find meaning in existence.

To the Lighthouse is informed by a strong sense of the chaotic nature of modern life. The three main characters are especially aware of the disorder around them and the complexity of their responses to that disorder. Disturbed by this confusion they strive to discern some pattern in existence and, if necessary, are willing even to impose a sense of order on the constant flux of daily life. Lily attempts to find stability and meaning through art, Mrs. Ramsay through social relationships, and Mr. Ramsay through intellectual pursuit. Each of these methods, its uses and limitations, is explored. No one way provides an "answer"; each is tainted by artificiality. But each offers some measure of comfort, some help in coping with existence.

Lily paints because she is driven by a sense of a "truth" which she must express in shapes and colors (236). But painting also offers a means of achieving order: Lily is one of a series of poets, painters, and thinkers in Virginia Woolf's novels who use their art and minds in an attempt to create a semblance of ordered stability out of life's formlessness.[3] A paintbrush is to her "the one dependable thing in a world of strife, ruin, chaos" (224). It is true that art gives Lily a way to escape from the pressure to marry or the needling of someone like Charles Tansley repeating, "Women can't paint, women can't write" (75). But art also gives her the answer to the "simple" question: "What is the meaning of life?" There is, Lily thinks, no single answer or sudden "revelation." Instead, there are moments which seem illuminated by a special significance, moments which are made permanent: "Mrs. Ramsay saying, 'Life stand still here'; Mrs. Ramsay making of the moment something permanent (as in another sphere Lily herself tried to make of the moment something permanent)." It is her painting which allows Lily to see that "in the midst of chaos there was shape; this eternal passing and flowing (she looked at the clouds going and the leaves shaking) was struck into stability" (240 - 41). She imagines a conversation with Mr. Carmichael in which he confirms her belief: " 'you' and 'I' and 'she' pass and vanish; nothing stays; all changes; but not words, not paint" (267). Therefore, it does not matter whether Lily's painting is hung in a hall or discarded under a sofa; like a poet's words, if it is an honest attempt to express some deeply felt "truth," it has served its purpose (267).

However the complexity of life may pain him, still Mr. Ramsay has "his work," and his work is an attempt to use rational, logical means to discover order. As he pushes out into the limits of human understanding, the chaos in which he dimly perceives a pattern nearly overwhelms him, but he continues to search for the next step, the "R" in a symbolic alphabet of knowledge in which he has with great effort reached "Q". He is sometimes laughable in his inflated sense of heroism, but his self-imposed task is worthy of respect. Mrs. Ramsay's order is social, the planning of dinner parties and marriages. At dinner she is a social artist, forming and sustaining the appropriate mood through careful arrangement (146 - 68). The candles, the food, the table, and above all, Mrs. Ramsay contribute to the creation of an "island" which is separate from the flux of ordinary life. The participants in the communion at the dinner find that they are at least temporarily in a protected and stable world. The language used in describing the dinner party is drawn from the fields of art and religion, confirming that Mrs. Ramsay's attempt to create order is like Lily's, and that the sense of unity achieved is distinct from the ordinary.

It is ironic that only Mr. Carmichael, nearly always pictured dozing in the sun, achieves what might be called success through his art. Mr. Ramsay will never reach "R" in the alphabet of philosophical research; Mrs. Ramsay's ordering is dependent upon a limited mortal life as her dinner parties end, marriages turn sour, and she must die. Lily's paintings are rarely completed, and even when they are they do not satisfy her and are not for display. But Mr. Carmichael's poetry becomes popular, because of the War. From the chaos of a world war comes both his creativity and an intensified need for the ordering power of art: "The war, people said, had revived their interest in poetry" (202).

Lily does not read Mr. Carmichael's poetry but assumes she knows what it must be like; it is she who tells us that in spite of Mrs. Ramsay's dreams Paul and Minta's marriage has failed. Mrs. Ramsay is hurt by her husband's insisting on facts at the expense of another's feelings; he is annoyed by her willingness to sacrifice truth to sympathy. Mr. Ramsay is antagonistic about art and terrifies Lily if he walks near when she is painting; she can understand his work only through an image—"a kitchen table . . . when you're not there" (38). Yet each one's approach is useful at some time, just as each of the three has limits. Mrs. Ramsay's tampering with time and reality needs the controlling influence of her husband's objectivity, and she knows this. He in turn recognizes that rigidly adhering to facts can cause pain. Each attempt to organize the flux of life may be an attempt to achieve the impossible, because life is disorderly and fleeting. When Lily "exchanged the fluidity of life for the concentration of painting" (237) she briefly finds a way out of the chaos, and can arrest the passing of time in one sense: what she reduces to her canvas will last. Only the subjective human can find shape and meaning in life and can order time, but in doing this the individual must be aware that all perceptions *are* subjective. Imagination and memory not only shape objective reality; they distort it. The very act of imposing order upon time may be a distortion. But the drive to discover pattern (and therefore find meaning) in existence is great.

The structure of the novel reinforces the idea that the chaos of life can be tentatively organized by human intervention. Without people there is no need to order time and no way to measure it. The little winds which nose around the house in the "entr'acte" can move slowly, "gently, for there was time at their disposal" (190). Because people can be aware of their ephemerality, to them the difference between one night and ten years is great. The use of brackets in this section of the novel underscores the relative unimportance of man's affairs, whether this means the death of the central character, or the outcome of World War I. But in contrast to this technical assertion of relative weight is the fact that people can change the apparent course of nature: the house *is* rescued from the destruction of time. Similarly, meaning can be found in the chaos of life, even if it is only in widely spaced moments. The unity at dinner disintegrates and Lily's painting will be hidden in the attic. Nonetheless, these moments have immediate impact and through memory some power to last.

It is significant that Mr. Ramsay's "work" involves a philosophical consideration of the ambiguities of existence. Andrew explains to Lily that Mr. Ramsay is involved in a study of "subject and object and the nature of reality" (38). *To the Lighthouse* is likewise a study of subject and object and the nature of reality, a study which explores the distinctions between an actual physical object and one seen, imagined, or remembered by a human being. It acknowledges that neither the object nor the human interpretation can be simply described. Interpretation (that is, subjective reality) seems to matter most. There is little direct action in the novel and some of that is set apart in brackets. External reality obtrudes upon subjective reality (thought, memory, interpretation) much as the fairy tale which Mrs. Ramsay reads to James intrudes upon her thoughts "like a bass gently accompanying a tune, which now and then ran up unexpectedly into the melody" (87). For example, in the first section of the novel, in nearly twenty pages of text, there are less than two hundred words, a total of half a page, of either directly quoted speech or description of action (even including words of attribution, such as "he said" or "she felt"). The rest comprises feeling, thought, and memory, and most of the memories in turn are about emotions and ideas, not actions or events.

The simplest relationship between subjective and objective reality is displayed in passages which acknowledge the influence of perception upon external reality. Mind time and clock time are kept distinct; manipulation of time is acknowledged and contained within the bounds of chronology. For example, the use of the explanatory "it seemed" indicates that even James is aware of his exaggeration when he considers the possible trip to the Lighthouse as "the wonder to which he had looked forward, for years and years it seemed" (9). Similarly, Nancy uses her imagination magically to change a tidal pool into the ocean, turn "minnows into sharks and whales, and cast vast clouds over this tiny world by holding her hand against the sun" (114). In each case the transformation of external reality is recognized as contrary to fact. Like memory or daydream, this is a conscious use of subjectivity. Mrs. Ramsay describes the nature of such excursions in time when she mulls at the dinner table over some acquaintances last seen years before (140): that world is a "dream land," an "unreal but fascinating place." Because what was then the future is now past and "the end of that story" is known, it is possible to live in such a world without fear or hurry. "It was like reading a good book again," being in a dream world where time is static and meaning circumscribed.

In this instance, Mrs. Ramsay's trip into the past is clearly contained within the boundaries of chronological time. But occasionally

Virginia Woolf uses flashback and reminiscence without marking the transition from the present by the traditional signalling devices. For example, the episode in which Charles Tansley first appears in detail seems initially to be a narration in external time (15 - 26). Like her husband, Tansley annoys Mrs. Ramsay by insisting that the trip to the Lighthouse will be postponed by bad weather: " 'There'll be no landing at the Lighthouse tomorrow,' said Charles Tansley . . . . Surely, he had said enough. . . . She looked at him. He was such a miserable specimen, the children said, all humps and hollows." From her children's opinion Mrs. Ramsay turns to her dislike of his absolute adherence to facts; next she considers the way her children all disappear "as stealthily as stags" after a meal. This apparently reminds her of a specific day in which Tansley had followed her into the drawing room when the meal was over. Because she thinks he was "feeling himself out of things," she invites him to join her on an errand in town. The following pages describe that walk with a directness and detail that make it seem to be occuring in the present rather than in Mrs. Ramsay's memory. And there is no obvious indication from the author that the incident is actually being remembered, not enacted. Even Tansley's "thoughts" are introduced as if truly known. However, the reader can follow the chain of thought which leads up to this lengthy reminiscence, as the entire episode is bounded in time by Tansley's comments as he stands near the window. The conclusion to the episode echoes the introduction: " 'No going to the Lighthouse, James,' he said, as he stood by the window . . . . Odious little man, thought Mrs. Ramsay, why go on saying that?" Although the traditional signalling devices to indicate the use of internal time are absent, the narrative can be followed with minimal difficulty because of Mrs. Ramsay's associative thought and the frame in clock time. But the difference between exterior and interior time is significant: external events occupy little space in the novel compared to the rich development of the response to those events. Neither "subject" nor "object" is denied, but the "reality" which matters most in *To the Lighthouse* is strongly colored by individual perception. As James thinks when he finally reaches the Lighthouse and can see that it is actually "stark and straight" with windows and laundry, although for years he has pictured "a silvery, misty-looking tower with a yellow eye," both pictures are accurate, both visions are "true": "for nothing was simply one thing" (276 - 77).

This recognition of multiplicity is tied in the novel to an intricate

interweaving of symbolic presentations of complexity: fifty pairs of
eyes to understand one person, various views of the Lighthouse,
multiple perceptions of apparently simple events. Rounded
characters engaged in timeless questions, a grace and intensity of
language, a significant form—all these elements make *To the
Lighthouse* one of Virginia Woolf's very best novels.

II   The Waves

Leonard Woolf preferred this novel to all of his wife's work
(AWD, ix), and it is an accomplishment unmatched by her other
novels. The very intricacy which makes it so interesting is also what
stands in the way of understanding or enjoying it. *The Waves* is not
an easy book to read, but it is worth the struggle.

The Waves is concerned with topics familiar from Virginia
Woolf's other novels—human relationships, personal values, subjective and objective reality, the function of art, the purpose of individual and human life. More than any of her other books it explores these topics through form. This is what makes the novel both
interesting and difficult. To understand what Virginia Woolf is saying
in this novel and to appreciate what she has done, it is necessary to examine her unique method of characterization, the use of a pattern to
supplement plot, the various functions of images and symbols, and
how these three major devices relate to each other.

The most superficial examination of *The Waves* reveals how unusual the book is: pages of lyric descriptive "prose-poems" in italics
alternate with chapters in which six seemingly disembodied
"voices" deliver monologues which are an experimental blend of
speech, thought, and the nonverbal content of the human mind. In
one sense the six are individuals. Bernard, Louis, Neville, Jinny,
Rhoda, and Susan are six separate people, with distinct bodies, personal interests, and individual lives. But they are united in a strange
intimacy, to form part of a potential whole. Each is representative
of some point-of-view or character type: Bernard is a potential
novelist, Jinny enjoys the sensuous life of the body, Rhoda is men-
tally unstable and, like Louis, insecure and afraid, Susan lives at one
with the natural world, Neville is a poet and homosexual. In-
dividually they reflect part of the range of human possibilities;
together with the silent Percival they symbolically create a single
complete person. Although he never speaks and he dies halfway

tl.rough the book Percival, the seventh character, is of great importance to the novel. He is a young man of action, a potential hero of the traditional type. His silence and his death suggest the failure of the realistic novel (structured around a hero who could take purposeful action) and the inability of the other six to form a complete human being or to represent the entire potential of human life. In this sense they may stand for modern man, no longer able to understand, let alone influence, the world.

The plot is easily summarized. The novel is a kind of group *Bildungsroman*, tracing the growth from infancy to maturity of six characters instead of the usual one. Direct action, however, is replaced with significant or representative moments often of symbolic actions, distorted by being refracted through the subjective glass of the interior monologues. In the first chapter, the six develop from infants to young children, apparently together at a boarding school. In the second, they separate into two groups as the boys attend one school (where Percival is introduced) and the girls another. Bernard and Neville (and Percival) are in college in Chapter III, although Louis, the best student, has been forced by financial reasons to take an office job. Meanwhile Susan is happy at her father's farm and Jinny and Rhoda are in London, the former enjoying the constant social rounds, the latter fearing and hating this life. In Chapter IV the six speakers and the ever-silent Percival reunite in London for dinner. Percival is the guest of honor, because he is soon to leave for India. The six struggle to define themselves for each other and if necessary against each other, but they also experience brief moments of intense union. The next chapter is the middle of the book, and in it three of the speakers respond to Percival's death in India: Neville who loved him, Bernard whose son has just been born, and Rhoda who is reminded by her friend's death of the ugliness and futility of life. Jinny, Susan, and Louis are silent. Chapter VI selectively presents only Louis, Susan, Jinny, and Neville, each asserting identity in a characteristic situation: Louis in his office thinks about poetry and about Rhoda, his lover; Susan is in her farmhouse with her children; Jinny is at a party, alert to the rich possibilities of experience; Neville is with his current lover, one of a series in his hopeless search for Percival. The passing of time is the dominant note of the next chapter which presents Bernard in Rome "shedding one of my life-skins" (306), Susan walking with her son and thinking "life stands round me like glass round the imprisoned reed" (309), Jinny carefully preparing to meet yet another young man, although she is painfully aware that she is no longer young, and the poet, Neville, like Jinny also with yet another young man. Louis is alone again, tracing the shape of words on a page; Rhoda is also alone, having left Louis because she "feared embraces" (318) as she fears life. The second reunion occurs in the eighth chapter. But Percival's absence, like the failure of Rhoda and Louis's love, emphasizes that loss and endings, not opportunities or beginnings, are what remain. The final chapter is Bernard's summary of the strange relationship and what it may mean. He asks, " 'Who am I?' I have been talking of Bernard, Neville, Jinny, Susan, Rhoda and Louis. Am I all of them? Am I one and distinct? I do not know" (377). And what is man, he asks, "the savage . . . who dabbles his fingers in ropes of entrail" or a heavenly creature with a body like "some cool temple," deserving "worship" (378)? At the center of life, where there should be an answer, there is only a "shadow," he feels: "Light floods the room and drives shadow beyond shadow to where they hang in folds inscrutable. What does the central shadow hold? Something? Nothing? I do not know" (379). These paradoxes bother not only Bernard; they are Virginia Woolf's questions and those of many writers who were her contemporaries.

In the nine chapters there is no narrator to offer answers to questions like these or even to give objective descriptions of characters or settings. Between chapters, however, are brief "prose-poems," a few paragraphs about the world outside the minds of the six speakers. The sun, the sea, the beach, a house and garden, and the birds in the garden are the elements which appear in some or all of the italicized sections which complement the chapters in a variety of ways. The prose-poems present a broad sweep of time, the movement from sunrise to sunset and from season to season, and thus through a mythic representation of natural development which parallels the "plot" of the novel: birth, growth, maturation, age, death. But the pattern is not simply linear. In the upward movement seeds of decay are implanted and in the downward movement, hints of renewal. At first the grey sea is indistinguishable from the sky, the birds barely chirp, the landscape is colorless. Then individual waves become distinct while flowers and fruit ripen; blue, green, silver, red, and yellow brighten the prose-poems. Later still the colors are those of the harvest, the waves pound firmly against the shore, the birds sing loudly in chorus or alone. Finally the colors fade, as darkness blends sky and sea in a silent world tipped with snow. Throughout, however, there is a counter-movement. The waves may be beautiful but they are also deadly; the birds sing in chorus or assert themselves aggressively, they fly "lovelily" or pick at the body of a worm until it festers; flowers bloom in color or waft "dead smells" as they decay; fruits ripen and then bloat and turn rotten, oozing thick excretions from split skin. The sun shines at noon in the interlude which introduces Percival's death. The ninth prose-poem is a mingling of seasons: there is snow in the mountains and darkness everywhere, but the trees are "in full summer foliage." Such intermixing suggests a kind of mythic progression, the cycle of birth, death, and renewal which ultimately is introduced into the main characters as well.

The device of the internalized dramatic monologues, each introduced by the tag "said Rhoda" or "said Neville," is one of the most striking features of *The Waves*. The characters do not literally speak to each other nor do they deliver standard soliloquies. On occasion the device provides a vehicle for communication much like dialogue. Usually stream-of-consciousness is subjective and marked by an individualizing style, but in these utterances the word choice and sentence structure are more or less the same. Only the characteristic interests and image patterns of each speaker mark one monologue from the next: Jinny, for example, notes city houses and streets, bright red and yellow silk dresses, and physical sensations, while Susan's words revolve around the green fields, small animals, and warm oven smells of her country home. The clusters of words used by each reveal outstanding traits. Neville repeats words like "formless," "neat," "perfection," and "order," suggesting his fussiness and precision. Similarly word choice underscores Susan's affinities with nature and elemental passions, Jinny's physical orientation, Rhoda's fear, Bernard's occupation with writing, and Louis's conflict between frustration in the present and fulfillment through a sense of life's continuity. Each thinks of language differently: to Jinny a word is fire-colored, to Susan words are natural objects like sand or pebbles, to Bernard they are alive; Neville delights in the orderly exactness of language while Jinny describes her use of language as careless. In fact, however, the form of all the dramatic monologues is strikingly similar. Sentence length and structure vary not from individual to individual, but from one time period to another. In childhood, for example, the soliloquies are short, the sentences are simple, and in the first monologues they display an identical syntax as well as a basic similarity of content: "I see a

ring . . .''; "I see a slab of pale yellow . . ."; "I hear a
sound . . .''; and so on. The sentences become more complex and
the number of sentences in each utterance grows as the children
grow. When the friends review their life together at the first dinner
they repeat the order of the first seven speeches in utterances
stylistically reminiscent of those early ones. Although sentences increase in length and complexity to reflect maturation, diction
remains essentially unchanged. Even in the first chapter, children
too young to bathe themselves employ such words and phrases as
"pendant currants like candelabra," "reprieve from conversation,"
and "surmount this unintelligible obstacle." The effect of this is to
make of the soliloquies a kind of mask, increasing the sense of unity
among the six and removing their speeches from the realm of everyday language.

The characters themselves, especially Louis and Bernard, talk
about a theory of horizontal and vertical unity among people which
also operates elsewhere in Virginia Woolf's work. For example,
Louis presents the idea of relationship through time by picturing
himself as a stalk whose "roots go down to the depths of the world":
"Up here my eyes are green leaves . . . Down there my eyes are the
lidless eyes of a stone figure in a desert by the Nile" (182). Bernard
and Susan know that children provide a link with the future. The
idea of a larger human community, "this omnipresent, general life"
(253), partly solves the problem of the transitory quality of life. For
the six speakers there is yet another unity, caused by a common personal past which gives them a shared fund of experiences and impressions. Bernard once says he is "a man of no particular age or
calling" (230), an assertion supported by the universalizing effect of
the novel's lack of explicit settings, physical descriptions, costum-
ing, or weather. The novel's general pattern (development from infancy to maturation) and its universalizing style emphasize the
characters' representative nature. The unity among the six is further
enhanced by their unconscious exchanges of identifying image
patterns, an indication of unusual intimacy. They share some images, such as a ring or circle which itself becomes a symbol of unity:
the image of "a chain whirling round, round, in a steel-blue circle
beneath" (270) describes a moment of communion at the first
dinner party, which is soon broken, so that "the circle is destroyed.
We are thrown asunder" (274). In addition each knows phrases and
images which the others use to describe to themselves actions,
appearances, responses, and thoughts, words and phrases which

have not been expressed in ordinary discourse. By thinking of one another these characters can bring each other into existence or in a different sense bring to the surface a different facet of the potentially complete human being they form together. With Bernard's comment, "Let me then create you. (You have done as much for me)" begins a series of soliloquies in which one speaker animates the next by thinking of him or her (233 - 47). Bernard concludes a monologue by thinking of Louis, who begins to speak in the next line and who ends with a description of Susan's simple existence, introducing Susan at her farm home. She in turn concludes with a picture of evening, first at her farm, then in the city, and with a memory of Jinny; the character who follows is Jinny, at evening, in the city. This is not ordinary human interaction but the author's attempt to indicate the unusually close unity among the six.

It is Virginia Woolf's belief that the need for communication is very strong. The use of the identifying tag "said X" in the monologues is curious but significant, because nothing is actually being "said." The word "thought," while also inexact, might be more easily accepted; but the novel's concern with the possibilities of communication explains the word choice. For all their strange unity and unusual communication, the characters are individuals too, and a tension between unity and separation is constantly maintained.

At various times the characters are more aware of their unity with others or their individual identity. When Louis signs his name, he thinks it is "clear, firm, unequivocal . . . my name. Clear-cut and unequivocal am I too" (291). But the sense of selfhood is not always so "firm." Bernard asks a universal question when he says, "What am I?"; he concludes "I am not one and simple, but complex and many" (227). Yet however complex they are, they are also distinguishable. For example, as a child Jinny kissed Louis. This experience is animating to Jinny, shattering to Louis, agonizing to Susan; Rhoda is oblivious of the event and Bernard is aware only indirectly at the time, although in his summary he notes that the kiss Jinny gave Louis lingers on his own neck, another instance of unconsciously shared feelings. A series of parallels and oppositions among the characters is established, some of which have already been noted. Only Bernard and Susan marry and have children; Rhoda and Louis are briefly lovers, while Neville and Jinny are alike in having a series of temporary partners, but different in that Neville's relationships are homosexual and all of his lovers are somehow one, an idealized Percival. Louis and Neville desire order and precision; Susan hates both. Rhoda is silent, nameless, faceless; in contrast, Bernard is a wordsmith and phrasemaker, multi-named (Byron, Hamlet, Napoleon, Shelley). Jinny and Susan are primarily aware of physical reality while Rhoda lives in a world of dream and Bernard in one of imagination.

Alternations of separation and unity are especially obvious at the two dinners, where the characters intensely feel both extremes. In instances of separateness such as their arrival at the first party, the characters' differences and sense of individuality are sharply delineated. They self-consciously, even brutally, assert contrasts in appearance, attitude, and background. This makes the moments of unity more striking. A strange sort of conversation occurs at the crests of the rising and falling waves of unity (268 - 70). Rhoda and Jinny's thoughts about their heightened sense perception lead to Louis's observation of "the roar of London." A siren he hears reminds Louis of a ship heading to sea and Neville, the next speaker, thinks of Percival who is leaving by ship for India. Next Bernard pictures India where Percival rides a "flea-bitten mare," an image Rhoda soon echoes. Then Louis thinks, "it is Percival . . . who makes us aware that these attempts to say, 'I am this, I am that,' which we make, coming together, like separated parts of one body and soul, are false." It is Percival who allows Louis to state overtly what the pattern of the preceding speeches has been demonstrating: while the characters remain separate individuals sitting around the table, they experience a moment of intense communion. There is no ordinary conversation, yet images and ideas are reflected from one mind to another. The soliloquies seem to reflect an experience (which includes conversation) as it sifts down into the characters' minds. No one really speaks of Percival "riding alone on a flea-bitten mare" or being the source of their unity, but all share thoughts of him, perhaps induced by a dinner table conversation of his possible future in India or perhaps merely the result of the mood established at this farewell party.

The most direct attempts at conversation occur between Rhoda and Louis at each party, but these are brief interchanges, extraordinary in form and content and, at the second party, indicative of the failure of their love. Louis starts the first conversation by calling directly, "Look, Rhoda"; then the two reflect each others' thoughts by echoing images, words, and phrases:

"Like the dance of savages," said Louis, "round the camp fire. They are savage; they are ruthless. They dance in a circle, flapping bladders. The flames leap over their painted faces. . . ."
"The flames of the festival rise high," said Rhoda. "The great procession passes . . . ." (272 - 73)

At the second party a similar interchange ends with Rhoda's overt recognition of failure: they have lost the possiblility of real communication, she says, for they "trust only in solitude and the violence of death and thus are divided." Louis echoes his agreement, "for ever . . . divided" (336). As he listens to an unreported conversation, Neville describes how conversation seems to occur here: "And so (while they talk) let down one's net deeper and deeper and gently draw in and bring to the surface what he said and she said and make poetry" (314). So in "dialogue" the soliloquies reveal what a net dipped into the mind might catch as the remnants of shared conversation and experience. Although the characters remain locked in parallel soliloquies, an intense communication sometimes seems possible.

In his summary Bernard attempts to review his life but discovers that it is intricately interwoven with the lives of the other characters, so that he cannot speak of himself alone. Neither is it possible to think of the six as a unit: they are one and yet separate. He insists upon the individuality of each; still, when he describes the process of individualization which they endured as children Bernard unconsciously and significantly uses one of Rhoda's private images, suggesting "we were all different" because "the virginal wax that coats the spine melted in different patches for each of us" (343,cf. 205). Such incorporation of the others' images and experiences into his thoughts is typical of Bernard's summary. He makes the meaning of this overt by noting "I do not altogether know who I am—Jinny, Susan, Neville, Rhoda, or Louis: or how to distinguish my life from theirs" (368); "nor do I always know if I am man or woman, Bernard or Neville, Louis, Susan, Jinny or Rhoda—so strange is the contact of one with another" (372).

The unity among the six reflects far more than a recognition of universal human needs and responses, but they do not simply feel themselves one. Bernard recalls that at the dinner parties, "We saw for a moment laid out among us the body of the complete human being who we have failed to be, but at the same time, cannot forget.

All that we might have been we saw; all that we had missed" (369).
The "complete human being" could be what the six together might
symbolize, or it could be Percival who was "complete" in an active,
potentially heroic way which the others admire. The funeral image
(the "body" which is "laid out among us") reflects Percival's death.
But the mock-heroic mode of Percival's presentation asserts his
more basic failure—the typically modern failure of the hero to act
in full accord with his potential. Percival is the necessary center of
unity at the first dinner; his very name invokes the knights in search
of the grail. Yet Bernard visualizes his future in India in words
which reveal both his desire for a hero and his fear that heroes do
not exist: "Behold, Percival advances; Percival rides a flea-bitten
mare, and wears a sun-helmet." When he helps to right a cart "the
multitude cluster round him, regarding him as if he were—what indeed he is—a God" (269). Percival may need protection from the
sun like an ordinary human, he may ride a horse worthy of Don
Quixote, and his death is likewise Quixotic (his horse falls and,
because a strap is loose, Percival is killed). Nonetheless he is also an
ideal, a "god" or hero.

The ambiguity contained in Percival's presentation and the uncertainty symbolized by the "central shadow" likewise infect the
novel's many images, dominated by water imagery.[4] The waves are
beautiful, a source of creativity and life, but they also have "odds
and ends, sticks and straws, detestable little bits of wreckage, flot-
sam and jetsam, floating on the oily surface" (363). As Neville steps
off the train which has carried him from school and thus symbolically steps into life, he thinks of "that chaos" as an ocean: "the huge
uproar" nearly engulfs him; he becomes "drawn in, tossed down,
thrown sky-high" (224). The immersion in life (the sea) is thus both
frightening and exciting. Water can be a source of life: Bernard first
becomes aware of the "arrows of sensation" when water is sponged
onto him (192). But Louis's repeated image of a "chained" beast
which stamps on the beach has merged into an image of the sea by
the fifth prose-poem. Here the "great beast" is chained, but it
remains potentially a destructive force. The prose-poems describe
broken boats left on the shore, while Susan recalls a drowning (205).
Even though Percival dies on land, Neville speaks as if Percival
drowned ("There was a surge; a drumming in his ears" [280]) and
his death makes Rhoda think of being "dashed like a stone on the
rocks," of sinking in "rough waters" (286). Yet Rhoda can also find
comfort in thinking of quiet, still pools and recognize that to men

marching in the desert water can be salvation (189). Because Rhoda wants to immerse herself in life but is afraid to, and fears yet invites death, the ambivalence toward water displayed in her images is especially suggestive.

Other images used by the characters and in the prose-poems confirm this sense of the complex, paradoxical nature of life and of man. The six characters are defined in part by analogies between human life and the waves, birds, and animals, and by an interplay of images between the prose-poems and the soliloquies. The analogies between birds and people are especially sharp, but people are also compared to water: each person is both an individual wave which crests just once and the elements of that wave which return to cycle through the tides; the second of these aspects is linked to "the unlimited time of the mind," the first to "that other clock," the chronological one (366).

Like the three main characters of *To the Lighthouse*, the six speakers search for a way to order life's chaos and thus are attracted to concepts which support the validity of "unlimited" mind time. Images of shapes, patterns, and designs suggest such order. For Bernard the "arbitrary design" of art seems useful but it too is limited. Life is "imperfect, an unfinished phrase" (373) and so may not be "susceptible . . . to the treatment we give it when we try to tell it" (362). Virginia Woolf's answer here is to challenge the order of the classic novel. She destroys the one potential hero by denying him speech and by surrounding him with mockery. There are some elements of the traditional plot here, even a sort of love entanglement—Percival loves Susan who loves Bernard who marries someone else. But conflicts which in an ordinary novel would be developed are here insignificant; the response is what matters, not the stimulus for that response. Actions are presented indirectly or not at all; such information as the characters' ages is casually introduced from time to time. To a surprisingly large degree Virginia Woolf has discarded the externals of the "materialistic" novel, but she cannot destroy all order. Then, as Bernard observes, the question must still be faced, "Why impose my arbitrary design?" (306). Virginia Woolf has not rejected selection and order; she has simply established new criteria for what should be selected and tried to use a "design" of growth and decay which, because of its natural and mythic analogies, and because its presentation is tentative, may seem less "arbitrary" than traditional plot.

Bernard's summary, which he calls a "story," is as "final" a "statement" as he makes, the statement for which he was "perpetually making notes in the margin of my mind" (307).[5] Without including "every known variety of man and woman" as he said his novel would (221), it comes close through the symbolic roles of the characters. In his summary, Bernard offers no answers: he is not sure who he is or what the truth may be. To make something symbolic, to give it order and form (as art does), is to make it "perhaps permanent" and "outside our own predicament," he notes, but is also to falsify it (349). There is no neat conclusion to "his" novel. Tiring, Bernard nearly ends his monologue with a sigh, "a last ripple of the wave," but suddenly he is renewed. As the waves "rise and fall and fall and rise again" (383), so too clouds "cover the stars, then free the stars, then cover the stars again" (381) in yet another suggestion of permanence. Bernard immediately internalizes these images, thinking "in me too the wave rises" (383). Describing dawn as a kind of universal rebirth, he uses words and phrases from the early prose-poems, underscoring the sense of circling back to a beginning. But he knows he is an elderly man who may be seeing city lights instead of dawn, the traditional symbol of renewal. When he heroically asserts that he will "ride" against "Death," the "enemy," he ironically invokes Percival, a mock-hero. So the novel ends in a burst of heroic rhetoric severely undercut by mockery, and with a complex, tentative suggestion of some kind of universal (but probably not personal) permanence. This conclusion accords with the dualistic nature of the rest of the book: man is beautiful and bestial, birth and death equally cause sorrow and joy, there is clock time on the one hand and mind time on the other, or nature and man, or external and internal reality, or mythic cycles and individual life—and all of these are supported by the division into prose-poems and monologues. Within the pattern, chaos still exists. As Bernard says, order is at best "a convenience" and may be "a lie," for underneath it there is always "a rushing stream of broken dreams, nursery rhymes, street cries, half-finished sentences and sights" (353 - 54). And this idea, like the other major themes, is displayed primarily through form in this most unusual novel.

Virginia Woolf's analysis of human feelings and relationships in *The Waves* is unusually fine, her sensitive understanding of man's attempts to find a way out of his loneliness and his confusion is superb. Thus, as significant a modernist milestone as this work is, it is not only because of its experimental nature or its successful interplay of form and meaning that *The Waves* is among Virginia Woolf's most important novels, but also its penetrating quality.

CHAPTER 6

Plot and Pattern

P LOTS don't matter," Virginia Woolf once wrote to Lytton Strachey.[1] This apparently bullheaded assertion makes sense if seen within the special context of Virginia Woolf's modernism. "Plots don't matter" because it is what goes on inside the characters that does. Virginia Woolf repeatedly challenges the kinds of ordering achieved by conventional plots. She suggests that the twentieth-century protagonist may no longer be capable of structuring his world or of taking direct and meaningful action: his world is too complex, he knows his perception may be inaccurate, he cannot understand himself, let alone the people around him. Traditionally plot is constructed from the conflicts the hero faces and the solutions he evolves; it builds to a climax as the conflict intensifies and concludes through the resolution. But many modernists believe that solutions may not be found and that the stability implied by resolution is false. Virginia Woolf does not entirely discard traditional plot, but she questions its validity (in *The Waves*, for example) and she constantly experiments with alternate designs. An early novel like *Night and Day*, in spite of its emphasis upon mental states, relies on a relatively conventional love story for its narrative structure, even reflecting Shakespearean comedy. *The Years* may appear a step backward from the experimental form of the four novels preceding it, in that it is a family saga organized chronologically. But a comparison with more traditional chronicles written at the same time (such as *The Forsyte Saga* by John Galsworthy or E. A. Bennett's *Clayhanger* trilogy) makes clear the differences. The conflicts which occur on center stage in the traditional novel are present but relegated to a far corner in *The Years*. The structure of *Between the Acts* depends upon an allegorical relationship between the macrocosm of world history (the pageant performed in the book) and the microcosm of a single family's life (scenes of which occur "between the acts" of the

119

pageant). Thus in both *The Years* and *Between the Acts* a symbolic pattern replaces plot as the main source of order.

I The Years

In *The Years* Virginia Woolf presents members of an upper-middle class English family, the Pargiters, at selected moments in their lives over more than half a century, from late in the Victorian era to just before World War II. The book is divided into eleven unnumbered chapters, each titled only with a year: 1880, 1891, and so on, up to the "Present Day." The births, marriages, career decisions, deaths, successes, and tragedies of three generations of Pargiters generally occur offstage, to be revealed in passing by the narrator or through dialogue. Each chapter presents a portion of an ordinary day, first as it affects the general population (time, season, weather, social or political conditions) and then narrowing to some of the family's special interests. Virginia Woolf wanted *The Years* to be "*The Waves* going on simultaneously with *Night and Day*," to modify the "representational" form and "compact" into it prose-poem "interchapters" (AWD, 191, 187, 189). There is an introduction to each chapter with reference wider than that of the body of the chapter, but it is not separated (as in *The Waves*), nor is it strictly universal or necessarily more symbolic than the rest of the chapter. For example, the first chapter opens with a description of the ever-changing "uncertain" spring weather which is noticed by "interminable processions of shoppers in the West end, of business men in the East." In the residential areas, young women servants prepared tea (3 - 4). Later on this April day, the Pargiters join together for such a tea. This section is typical of the stage direction passages. Generally descriptions of city or country, day or night, appear in both the introduction and the body of each chapter; specific characters and even facts about events in the lives of the Pargiters are present in the introductions; an omniscient narrator dominates point-of-view in both. The data derived from the "interchapters" and the narrative itself create a skeleton of the lives of Colonel Abel Pargiter, his children and grandchildren, his brother Digby, Digby's wife Eugénie and their children and grandchildren, the Malones (cousins), and a few friends and servants.

The novel opens in the spring of 1880 on the day Abel Pargiter's wife, Rose, dies after a long illness. Edward is the only one of the

Pargiter children who is not living at home. Eleanor at twenty-two
is the oldest; Morris is training to be a lawyer; defiant Delia dreams
of the Irish leader Parnell; Milly tries to fill her mother's place at
tea; and Martin and Rose, the youngest, are about twelve years old.
Colonel Pargiter spends some time with his mistress, although he
considers their situation "sordid" (7): he is controlled by her comparative youth as she is made subservient by the roles they have
adopted. The last person of significance is Crosby, the maid to the
Pargiter family until their house is sold nearly forty years later.
After Mrs. Pargiter's death, the focus shifts to Edward at Oxford,
where Eleanor earlier wrote to him. For the next transition, the setting remains the same (the University) but the people change:
Professor Malone and his family are introduced, calling attention to
Kitty Malone, who is loved by her cousin Edward but is driven to
escape the life of a university town. Announcement of Mrs.
Pargiter's death (the Malones' "Cousin Rose") provides the most
obvious link, and the final section of the chapter is set in London for
her funeral.

Eleven years pass before "Chapter Two." Kitty is married and
lives in the country; Milly is married to a rather dull man whose sole
interest is hunting; Edward and Morris are established in their
careers and Eleanor in hers—caring for her father and a variety of
business and social ventures. On this October day in 1891, Eleanor
works on the family budget, attends a committee meeting, has
lunch with her father, reads a letter from Martin in India, observes
Morris arguing a case at court, and notices a newspaper announcement of Parnell's death "yesterday" (120). (This announcement
makes it possible to deduce the exact date: the day after Parnell's
death was October 6.) At the same time, Colonel Pargiter sees the
same headline. The scene shifts to Digby Pargiter's servant, who
answers the bell to find Colonel Pargiter at the door. Although the
Colonel wants to talk with his sister-in-law about his mistress (as he
had earlier wanted to discuss her with Eleanor), he instead joins the
family celebration of his niece Maggie's birthday. Discussion of the
family and politics further acquaints the reader with the lives and
times of these representative individuals.

The longest gap (sixteen years) occurs between the second and
third chapters. On a midsummer night in 1907 Eugénie, Digby, and
Maggie attend a party while their other daughter, Sara (in bed on
doctor's orders) listens to dance music from another party and
glances at her cousin Edward's translation of *Antigone*.

A cold windy March day sets a changed mood for the next chapter ("1908"). Martin rings the doorbell at Digby's house but the house has been sold following the deaths of Digby and Eugénie.[2] Martin next stops at the family home where Eleanor and their father still live. Some things remain unchanged by the passage of time: Crosby still answers the door, and Eleanor still frays the wick with a hairpin hoping to make the tea kettle boil faster. But the Colonel has aged noticeably and Eleanor has grown absent-minded. As is increasingly true in the later chapters, the characters reminisce, usually about events shown earlier in the book. This time, Martin and Rose find a bond between them in their memories of childhood squabbles; later this will seem to be their only bond.

In 1910, on the day of the King's death (Edward VII died on May 7), Rose has lunch with Maggie and Sara who share an apartment in a poor section of London. Maggie still goes to parties, though she now makes her own clothes; Sara is an eccentric. After lunch Sara attends a meeting with Rose. As they walk, the point-of-view shifts to an old flower-seller at whose stall "two ladies" stop. That the "tall lady" with a "cackle of laughter" is Sara and the "short and stout" one Rose is ascertained only when the narrator resumes an omniscient point-of-view (174 - 75). At the meeting the perspective again changes so that Eleanor's sense prevails; she fails to recognize Sara. Later Eleanor accepts a ride in Kitty's car (thus reflecting historical change: in earlier chapters she rides in horse-drawn cabs or on a bus). Next the opera is seen through Kitty's eyes, after she leaves Eleanor at the tube (subway) station. In the final scene a cry floats from the street to Maggie and Sara's apartment: "The King's dead" (191).

Eleanor visits Morris in August 1911, as she has for many years, but now her father is dead and the family home is closed. At fifty-five she is "labelled," inaccurately she thinks, "an old maid who washes and watches birds" (203). Eleanor's conversation with Celia reveals more family history: Rose's political activism has led to a court trial though not to prison (this time), Maggie has married a Frenchman, and so on. Two of Morris and Celia's children (North and Peggy), and a guest, Sir William Whatney, increase Eleanor's awareness of the passage of time. Still she feels that she is more like the young people than her former admirer, Sir William, because her life "was beginning" (213). For the first time she is free of responsibility for anyone other than herself.

Eighteen months later she has not lost this new energy, as is apparent when she and Crosby reminisce on a snowy January night. To the old servant, however, the sale of the family home is an ending: she moves to a room, bringing mementos from her earlier life and even the family dog. But the dog soon dies, and except for seeing Martin weekly (when she picks up his socks to wash), she is isolated from the past, and has no hope for the future. Martin's view dominates the last scenes, as he thinks there is "trouble brewing" in the world and that even at home, all is lies: his father lied about his mistress and now Martin lies to escape Crosby.

A spring day in 1914 is the setting for the next scene, one of the last ordinary days before the outbreak of World War I. Links in this chapter are underscored by references to time, much as in *Mrs. Dalloway*. At 11:00 Martin goes to St. Paul's, at 1:00 a man feeds pigeons in front of the Cathedral, and as the bells fade Martin walks out to where the man and pigeons are, to encounter Sara carrying a prayer book. After lunch they meet Maggie with her baby in the Park. While Sara sleeps, Maggie and Martin talk about the past and their families. In the evening Martin attends a dinner party at Kitty's, though he is convinced that the party will fail. His cynicism is apparent even to Kitty who fears she is not a successful hostess and is hurt that Eleanor refused her invitation. The party breaks up early, allowing Kitty to catch a night train to her country home. The ride is an adventure, and in the country she is comfortably at ease. When she arrives the house is quiet, "everything . . . shrouded and shut up." Although she is aware that "all passes, all changes," that she owns nothing of what she sees, nonetheless Kitty is content. For her "time had ceased," the future seems to lie open to her and to a harmonious world (276 - 78). The introduction to this chapter first describes such a peaceful country scene and then the vibrant, noisy city; the body of the chapter reverses that movement, from the crowded streets, parks, and parties of London to a solitary person lying in the grass. This peace is destroyed, however, by the opening of the next chapter.

The bleakness of a world at war is shown in the setting of the chapter headed "1917." The dark winter night is made darker by the blackout: no lights show on the street or shine from windows; a bus is "a great form" whose "lights were shrouded with blue paint" and whose silent passengers huddle together, "cadaverous and unreal" (300). Maggie and Renny (her husband's name has long been Anglicized) have invited Eleanor, Sara, and a friend (Nicholas) to dinner. During the meal an air raid begins, so the group eats in the cellar, bundled in blankets against the damp. They keep track of where the bombers strike by the intensity and spacing of the crashes. When it appears that they are safe until the next night's raid, they joke to forget about the war. But the bitterness in Renny's statement, " 'They're only killing other people' " (293), shows that forgetting is impossible. Their talk after the raid reveals a lot to Eleanor, whose point-of-view prevails: Renny's discomfort that he is not directly involved in the war effort, Nicholas's homosexuality (announced by Sara with a freedom impossible in 1880 and still somewhat disquieting to Eleanor), her own recognition that Renny is someone she would have liked to marry and that she resents those effects of time and chance which prevented her from finding the happy marriage she pictures Renny and Maggie to share (299). Thus in personal as in national life, loss dominates this section.

When the end of the war is announced in the next chapter ("1918") there is no rejoicing. This, the book's shortest chapter, is Crosby's and she is too conscious of age and misery to respond to the booming guns asserting victory. Even the weather reiterates the exhaustion at war's end: it is a damp November day, described in such pejorative words as "greasy," "deadened," and "growl."

The novel now skips from the end of one war to the prelude of another in the final and longest chapter, entitled "Present Day." References to the familiar blurry newspaper picture of "a fat man gesticulating," a man Eleanor calls a "damned . . . bully," suggest the time is during the Fascists' rise to power. Eleanor can hate Hitler and Mussolini as she does, her niece Peggy thinks, because that "wonderful" older generation had faith in "the things that man had destroyed." Eleanor confirms this when she tells Peggy that the new war "means the end of everything we cared for," including such abstractions as "freedom and justice" (330 - 32). But Peggy and her generation feel that the earlier war had already changed that world. In this chapter Peggy and Eleanor gather with three generations of Pargiters for a party Delia gives: a kind of summing up. Memory and possibility, the past and the future, change and permanence, age and youth are the major themes of the reunion as they have been of the novel.

Early in the chapter Peggy's brother, North, visits Eleanor, finding her with Nicholas, who is now furnished with the surname Pomjalovsky, "called Brown for short" (307). Eleanor, Nicholas, and Sara, their apartments and their city are all seen first through North's eyes, and after fifteen years of solitary farming in Africa he is an acute, somewhat distanced observer. Eleanor ignores her guests to show North her new shower, Nicholas talks about the psychology of great men (the same topic that interested him in 1917), eccentric Sara still lives in near-squalor. London seems noisy and hurried to North, but Eleanor also finds the degree of change disorienting: since the 1880's airplanes, telephones, hot water, the wireless, showers, electricity, and automobiles have all been introduced to her life and thus to the novel. About a third of the chapter alternates between Eleanor and Peggy either at Eleanor's apartment or en route to the party, and Sara and North dining in Sara's rooms. The two "Miss Pargiters" discuss the past, Peggy feeling that old age is memories, opening "endless avenues" and enchanting—but safely past—doors, while Eleanor envies Peggy's generation their "more interesting" lives (332 - 33). Meanwhile North and Sara share undercooked mutton and spotty fruit for dinner while talking about their years of correspondence. Peggy and Eleanor's arrival at Delia's party signals a shift to the somewhat larger society of the Pargiter family together. Point-of-view is variously limited to Eleanor, the oldest living Pargiter, and to Peggy or North representing the younger generation. Peggy is what Eleanor could never be, a professional career woman, and North sees his family afresh after his long absence.

Quick vignettes reintroduce many characters. The specific details of individual lives—that Kitty is a widow, or that Milly has grown very fat—matter less than the pattern of continuity. North thinks about Milly and her husband: "The men shot, and the women . . . broke off into innumerable babies. And those babies had other babies," and finally, mocking his own vision, he adds "the other babies had—adenoids" (375). That there may be such "a pattern; a theme, recurring, like music . . . a gigantic pattern, momentarily perceptible" gives Eleanor "extreme pleasure" (369), perhaps because it confirms her faith in the future and her belief that life is always just starting. The constant imposition of the past through memory supports this notion; even the room where the party occurs had been the setting for some of the meetings Eleanor and the others attended. The pattern is not mere repetition, however, for it includes the possibility of progress. They believe in the potential for "a new world" in which the human race may "grow to maturity" (422 - 26). Yet this is the eve of another world war as much as it is the dawn of a new world. When the caretaker's children enter, symbolizing the infants of the new era, they are at first silent. Induced at last to sing, the children "burst" into a "distorted and un-intelligible" song, which for all its hideousness still seems "beautiful" to the adults. The song ends in mid-verse, leaving the confused adults unsure of how to respond or what to think about this portent of the future (429 - 31). As the novel moves toward conclusion, the party breaks up (432 - 35). For a moment "the old brothers and sisters" form a group outlined against the window like statues "carved in stone." However brief, this serves as one more symbol of permanence, like the dawn which makes the world outside look "clean swept, fresh and virginal." Eleanor watches a young couple across the street as the man opens the door and the pair stands briefly on "the threshold" not just of a new home, it appears, but of a new world. This series of symbolic acts makes the novel end more optimistically than any other by Virginia Woolf. The optimism carries through to the concluding sentence, suggesting one of those rare moments of personal integration when man and his world seem in harmony: "The sun had risen, and the sky above the houses wore an air of extraordinary beauty, simplicity and peace." This belief in stability and order shimmers like a lovely rainbow and like the rainbow (for both characters and author) will fade quickly into the clouds of reality.

The question of pattern which Eleanor and the others raise is partly answered by the structure of the novel. There is little "plot" in the sense of specific conflicts and resolutions or a rise in tension to a climax followed by a gradual fall. What is emphasized instead is a pattern, the repetition of seasons and events from year to year. The oldest people die, their children and grandchildren give birth to yet another generation. No amount of external change can alter basic human needs and actions, which are repeated in all the years. In this pattern of continuity, the Pargiters serve as representatives of human life, the family of man. It may be, as Sara says, that there is nothing "ordinary" about a family "going on and on and on," but in their symbolic role they are as ordinary as Rose insists: "a large family, living in a large house" (168 - 69). In each generation there is a soldier (Abel, Martin, North); in each there are siblings bound by intense love and jealousy (Abel, Digby, and Eugénie, Martin and Rose, Peggy and North); in each there is a scholar or scientist (Professor Malone, Edward, Peggy), and so on. Such set descriptions, of course, are labels and like most of Virginia Woolf's characters, Eleanor and North object to labelling. As North says, such "little snapshot pictures of people left much to be desired"

(317). Once again Virginia Woolf is arguing that there are patterns
and people can be symbolic, but there is also the flux of the "here
and now" in which each person is isolated and alone.[3]

What it means to be an individual and how individuals can know
each other concern the characters in this novel as in other Woolf
novels. Maggie echoes Bernard when she asks, "Am I that, or am I
this? Are we one, or are we separate" (140), and Peggy sounds like
Maggie when she ponders her relationship with Eleanor: "Where
does she begin, and where do I end? . . . They were two living people . . . two sparks of life enclosed in two separate bodies. . . . But
what is this moment; and what are we?" (334). After seventy years
of asking herself such questions, Eleanor is no nearer the answer.
She realizes that as difficult as it is to describe her life, it is much
harder to describe another's (369). Like Eleanor, when her self-
conception does not quite match the image of her held by someone
she is with, Rose thinks of herself as "two people at the same time"
(169, cf. 176). This is further complicated by the fact that the same
person seems so different to two other people (154). There appears
to be no possibility of understanding another fully or making
yourself understood. And "this half knowing people, this half being
known" is very "uncomfortable," as North recognizes (313).

There are two reasons for this: first, that Virginia Woolf insists on
the inherent complexity of each individual's inner being, and second, that she presents characters as if each is not simply an isolated
individual. That is, she probes her characters as modern psychology
makes possible and at the same time she explores her special theory
of human continuity. Eleanor feels that her life is equally her
father's, her brothers', or her friend's life, and when Nicholas
appears it seems as if "a sunk part of her" rose to "the surface"
(367 - 68). One piece of support for this idea comes from the use of
motifs in the novel. Some events are crystallized into images which
recur as reminders of a personal past or as means of character identification (the white face which haunts Rose, for instance, or the
song Martin sings). But other images (the violet-sellers, fraying the
wick to make the kettle boil) are shared by several characters. The
one most extensively developed is of the pigeons crooning. Kitty,
Eleanor, and Sara all interpret the sound in the rather unusual for-
mulation "Take two coos, Taffy. Take two coos."

Many of the characters are similarly conscious of two worlds existing at once. Past and present intermingle for Eleanor (166 - 67),
the immediate and eternal are brought into focus for her by

Parnell's death (114). Both worlds matter. Structure reveals the
world of pattern: continuity, permanence, and symbol. But in *The
Years* Virginia Woolf makes the everyday world of the "here and
now" far more real than in *The Waves*. The characters stand firmly
on hard pavement in shoes which may sometimes be too tight (as
Milly's are). For all their symbolism these are also ordinary people
in whom ordinary human traits can readily be seen. As a result, the
novel is unusually accessible to the reader.

Virginia Woolf found *The Years* an exceptionally difficult novel
to write.[4] Leonard Woolf thought it her "worst book," although he
hid this opinion from her because of her severe doubts and her increasing illness.[5] But the newspaper reviews were generally
favorable, and the reading public agreed, making it her most
successful book, a best seller in the United States. Its popularity
may be attributed to its realistic surface, its comparatively straight-
forward presentation of character, and its relative freedom from
decorative language or subtle hints of hidden meanings. *The Waves*
and *Between the Acts* are the two novels most like it in theme; they
are more difficult but they also have more to offer.

II   Between The Acts

Between the Acts is Virginia Woolf's last novel, one of her best,
and probably her bleakest.[6] The entire action encompasses just
about a day, but the chronological reference is nearly infinite. All
the time man has known, however indirect that knowledge may be,
is compressed into an allegorical pageant and the briefly glimpsed
lives of a very few people. Three generations of the Oliver family
reside at Pointz Hall, a country estate not far from London:
Bartholomew Oliver, his widowed sister Lucy Swithin, his son Giles,
Giles's wife Isa, and their son and daughter. About this nucleus
revolve various others—a butler and cook, nursemaids, a delivery
boy from the village, and Mrs. Manresa and William Dodge, unexpected luncheon guests. In the afternoon an event occurs of some
importance to the village, the annual pageant which introduces
numerous villagers and local gentry as actors and audience, with the
author, Miss La Trobe, to direct the play and the Rev. G. W. Streatfield to summarize its meaning.

The first two scenes establish the novel's most important topics:
the essential loneliness of the individual, and its apparent contradic-
tion—the continuity of past and present, of man and his world.

Rupert Haines (a "gentleman-farmer") and his wife talk with "Old" Mr. Oliver about a cesspool to be built in the neighborhood, at a site "on the Roman road." The novel occurs at such a time and place that it is possible to ride in an airplane in order to observe signs of the distant past: "the scars" left by the ancient Britons and Romans, by the Elizabethans, and by farmers during the Napoleonic wars. Even individual families have lived in the same location for generations, in some cases (like Mrs. Haines) for centuries, with family graves in the church yard for proof. In contrast, the Olivers are relative newcomers, having lived in Pointz Hall "only something over a hundred and twenty years," with a portrait of "an ancestress of sorts" and a few family mementoes as proof of their place in history (7). Although Haines and his wife say little and do less, they unwittingly introduce the second main theme. Isa, whose relation with her husband is a complicated mixture of love and hate, is attracted to Rupert Haines, usually referred to simply as "the man in grey." This reference underscores his personal insignificance to Isa; to her Haines is a fantasy symbol, much as Katharine Hilbery is at first to Ralph Denham. At some only partly conscious level, Mrs. Haines is aware of Isa's sexual response to Haines, so she is also tense. Isa is domestic, sophisticated, and civilized, but at the same time sensual, childish, and brutal; although frustrated she is willing to cause frustration in others. Like someone with a toothache she wants a "cure." At thirty-nine she is "the age of the century" (19), and an apt symbol for the confusions of her age.

From this small group and intense opening, the novel contracts still further, so that the next morning begins with Lucy Swithin awakening alone in her room. Gradually the focus widens to take in first other members of the household and shortly later Mrs. Manresa and William Dodge. Mrs. Manresa is a middle-aged woman, "oversexed, overdressed," rather vulgar, but her exuberance is uncontrived; she is a "wild child," unashamed, as natural as the air (37 - 43, 55). William is a nervous "gentleman" who seems an outsider, perhaps because he may be an artist or poet or perhaps because of his homosexuality. Isa feels drawn to the alien William, Giles and Mrs. Manresa feel a mutual physical attraction; within these parameters the afternoon wears on towards the pageant in alternating tension and quiet. But even the periods of quiet display numbness rather than peace.

Finally the villagers assemble for the pageant. Isa and Mr. Oliver explain to Mrs. Manresa and William that the director "makes everyone do something," and that their part is to be the audience: "a very important part too." At this the only partly addled Mrs. Swithin slips in, "also, we provide the tea" (58). The pageant attempts to trace the history of England through some of the major periods of literature, beginning with a little girl symbolizing England's birth, rapidly moving to the Age of Chaucer, the reigns of Queen Elizabeth (Shakespeare's time), Queen Anne ("reason holds sway" [123]), and Queen Victoria. During each scene, villagers move across the stage, representing the first settlers in England, then the Canterbury pilgrims, and so on, as they chant words which gradually become more audible. For the Elizabethan age the villagers produce a play within a play. The actual audience (as opposed to the villagers who cluster around the stage-Elizabeth pretending to be an audience) can scarcely follow the plot, which is as convoluted as any real Renaissance play. Isa thinks that if "the plot was only there to beget emotion," then the details do not "matter"; still she wants to know what is happening on stage as well as off stage, in the interactions within the audience. An intermission breaks the emotion just being generated and the spectators separate to the plaintive call of a record: "The music chanted: *Dispersed are we.* It moaned: *Dispersed are we.* It lamented: *Dispersed are we*" (95). After the "interval," the pageant resumes with a clever imitation of a Restoration comedy, replete with the concerns (sex, money) and intrigues typical of the genre. Another interval is succeeded by scenes from the nineteenth century, emphasizing the divided nature of Victorian England: exploitation of the poor, prejudice, and hypocrisy on the one hand; social reform, prosperity, and progress on the other. Finally the pageant is brought up to the "Present Time. Ourselves" (177 - 88). As the spectators nervously wait, they feel "caught and caged," "exposed." They find it acceptable that the pageant's author understands the Victorians and the even more distant Elizabethans, but that she might know the present English people, those sitting in the audience, is "ridiculous." Miss La Trobe's intention to "try ten mins. of present time" and thus expose the audience to reality nearly fails ("reality too strong," she mutters in shorthand) when it suddenly rains. The rain was "all people's tears, weeping for all people," "sudden and universal." When the rain stops "a fresh earthy smell" rises from the grass. Once again, Miss La Trobe thinks, nature has "taken her part," for the audience responds to the rain in a manner she feels appropriate. Next comes a symbolic presentation of what is described by the note-taking journalist as "Civilization . . . in ruins; rebuilt . . . by human effort." That effort includes the League of Nations; when juxtaposed with the audience's talk of war this underscores the irony in what is called a "flattering tribute to ourselves." As the final action village children run out carrying makeshift mirrors to reflect the faces of the audience. A nose, a skirt, a pair of pants, one face: "Ourselves? But that's cruel. To snap us as we are, before we've had time to assume . . . . And only, too, in parts. . . . That's what's so distorting and upsetting and utterly unfair." In such fragments the audience reacts to this scene from the Present Time, this unrehearsed and unflattering picture of "ourselves." Only Mrs. Manresa has the confidence unblinkingly to confront herself, and this supposed child of nature uses the mirror to apply cosmetics which later at sunset look artificaly "plated" on her skin (202). Mr. Streatfield concludes the pageant by attempting to summarize its meaning and by collecting money for the "illumination of our dear old church" (193), with a pun he probably does not intend.

One way of interpreting the novel's title is to consider the pageant as the interruption in the drama of real life, so that the pageant's scenes occur "between the acts" of the marriage of Giles and Isa, the staging of parent-child conflicts, sibling rivalry, possible infidelities, and so on. On the other hand, if the "acts" are considered those of the pageant, then "between" those acts it is the audience's turn to become actors. Before the play Mrs. Swithin shows William the house. During the first interval, the audience gathers in the old barn for tea. Here William observes Isa's face changing as she assumes different roles with her son or her husband, and Mrs. Manresa is able to draw Giles in, "making him feel less of an audience, more of an actor" (108). Earlier she compares him to "the surly hero" of the pageant, while she is its queen (93). The characters are not always described in such overtly theatrical terms, but even action presented directly has an audience. The interplay between Giles and Mrs. Manresa is observed by Isa who sees "the Manresa in his wake" and predicts a later bedroom scene of explanation and ill will (110). She seems unaware of how Giles postures, seeking her admiration. When Isa shows William the greenhouse she is aware of thereby rebuffing Giles, and William watches Isa's reactions to note that he and she can talk freely together because there is no sexual potential to create tension. The second interval is (or is made to seem) shorter, perhaps because by now the pageant is beginning to have its effect on the audience, some of whom remain seated, feeling as if their identities were "floating unattached." Giles nonetheless invites Mrs. Manresa to the greenhouse, even though he is aware that there might be "consequences" (149 - 50). Most of the conversation in the next interval revolves around the play, perhaps suggesting the increasing involvement of audience and actors, or perhaps merely resulting from the subject matter of the recent scenes: parents and grandparents of members of the audience were Victorians; some of the older spectators grew up in the nineteenth century. Still, when Isa asks, " 'Were they like that?' " she looks at Mrs. Swithin "as if she had been a dinosaur or a very diminutive mammoth." Anyone who lived during Queen Victoria's reign must be "extinct" (174). The boundaries between the last interval and the final scene (Present Time), are undefined and "Present Time" is both the pageant's end and part of reality. After Mr. Streatfield's explanatory and fundraising speech, the audience leaves by foot or car, the actors return to their usual garb, and Mrs. Manresa and William take their leave. Attention briefly focuses on Miss La Trobe, unhappy (as always) after the performance. Although "glory possessed her—for one moment," and although she feels she has offered a "gift" through the play, still "she had suffered triumph, humiliation, ecstacy, despair—for nothing" (209 - 10). But this is not her last play; rather, "another play always lay behind the play she had just written" (63). As she sits alone and lonely in a crowded pub, she begins to think of that new play: "It would be midnight; there would be two figures, half concealed by a rock. The curtain would rise" and the two actors would speak words that she can already hear (210 - 12). Meanwhile the family, reduced after dinner to the four adults, talk quietly about that afternoon's play, though no two of them saw the same thing (213 - 19). Isa continues to reject Giles's attempts at contact (attempts presented in unusually direct sexual images: for example, Giles offers his wife a banana "with its sheaf sliced in four, exposing a white cone . . . . She refused it. He stubbed his match on the plate. Out it went with a little fizz"). But after Mr. Oliver and Mrs. Swithin go to sleep, Giles and Isa will enact the first scene in Miss La Trobe's new play: "Alone, emnity was bared; also love. Before they slept, they must fight; after they had fought, they would embrace. From that embrace another life might be born." The two are like the "dog fox" and "vixen" or "dwellers in caves," as significant, timeless, and basic as life itself. They confront each other in the darkened room, appearing "enormous" as they assume their archetypal roles. Finally, "the curtain rose. They spoke."

There are no clear boundaries between the pageant and life outside of the pageant. Just as there is no absolute division between the literal Giles and Isa in Pointz Hall at night and the symbolic Giles and Isa who (in Pointz Hall or in Miss La Trobe's new play) stand for the essential man and the essential woman, so there is no obvious point at which the play begins, and at its end the spectators have become the actors. Even the language of the pageant invades that of the audience, so that their thoughts contain bits of rhyme and a plethora of rhetorical devices. That the theater and reality are not separate is an idea carried out through the involvement of birds and weather, the sounds of nature and airplanes in the pageant. It is not just that the audience may hear the same birds in the scenes of the pageant as between the acts. At times the real world intervenes directly into the dramatic one. During the pseudo-Restoration comedy, for instance, a record "gently stated certain facts which everybody knows to be perfectly true"—among them, that after labor comes rest in the cool peace of evening: this statement is reiterated in nature by the setting sun and merging colors of the evening sky. Perhaps Miss La Trobe timed the scenes to ensure this occurence. But the most clever author could not guarantee that the cows, by stepping forward and then standing still, would provide a "triple melody" in which the audience is enfolded (133 - 34). Nor could she have arranged the sudden shower which saves the end of the pageant, or that the cows' "yearning bellow" should sound like "the primeval voice" and thus maintain an appropriate mood when the chorus of villagers cannot be heard (140). The sense that nature and man are in constant touch is further heightened by the sheer volume of natural images in the novel: flowers, cows, fish, trees, wind, rain, sun, butterflies, and especially birds. There are over fifty references to birds alone, either directly present (seen or heard) or indirectly mentioned, sometimes to create comparative links between people and nature ("goose-like eyes," for instance). A sampling ranges from pigeon and woodpecker to swallow and swan, even to some "prehistoric birds" in Mrs. Swithin's favorite book, an *Outline of History.*

But the pageant and its interaction with the world between the acts suggest even more strongly that there are links between all peo-

ple of all times. The chorus of villagers which appears in each scene
chants a refrain which mirrors the gradual unfolding of the
pageant's theme:

Digging and delving . . . for the earth is always the same, summer and
winter and spring; and spring and winter again; ploughing and sowing,
eating and growing; time passes. . . . (125)
All passes but we, all changes . . . but we remain forever the
same . . . . (139)

Mr. Streatfield offers his interpretation of the pageant's "meaning"
or "message" after appropriate apologies for his attempt. He is
"puzzled," he admits, yet feels the play suggested inherent human
unity: "Each is part of the whole. . . . We act different parts; but
are the same." If, he adds, this is true and it is true "that nature
takes her part," how can we "dare . . . limit life to ourselves?"
Even the village idiot is "part of ourselves," though a part we do
not like "to recognize," as one in the audience mutters (191 - 94).
Mr. Streatfield's explanation is not needed. At least some members
of the audience recognize the "message" far earlier than his summing up. Mrs. Swithin is primed to understand this pageant
because it accords with her theory of life. She says of the swallows in
the barn, "they come every year . . . the same birds" (101); her
thoughts are filled with images of the prehistoric past, apparently
her favorite part of her favorite book. So it is not surprising to hear
her say that there never were "such people" as the Victorians; "only
you and me and William dressed differently" (175). But she is not
even the first to note this theme. Fragments of conversation during
the first interval reveal the beginnings of recognition even as they
echo Virginia Woolf's attitude towards the importance of the internal rather that the external in human nature: "D'you think people
change? Their clothes, of course. . . . But I meant ourselves"
(120 - 21).
    That people do not change or at least that life has continuity is in-
sisted upon in the novel. Mr. Oliver recognizes that Isa "continued
him" through her children, making it possible for him to have a
future (18). Not only is the pageant repeated annually but so is the
talk surrounding it: Isa has "heard the same words" over and over,
she thinks; "every year they said, would it be wet or fine; and every
year it was—one or the other" (22). The villagers have been
"stationed" for three centuries "in that one corner of the world"

(27). Though the Olivers could only trace their ancestry some two or three hundred years, the Swithins "were there before the Conquest" and the families whom the delivery boy serves have names which "like his own, were in the Domesday Book" (30 - 31). In fact, had the author of an old guidebook called roll at the pageant, half the audience could have answered " 'I'm here, in place of my grandfather or great-grandfather' " (75). Pointz Hall itself reiterates the thesis that change is superficial, for it still has its pre-Reformation chapel, though now the chapel is used as a larder, "changing . . . as religion changed" (32). Behavior changes (today Mr. Oliver bows over Mrs. Manresa's hand whereas earlier "he would have kissed it" [38]), but the fundamental human emotions and needs and the interplay between people and nature remain.

For all its bleakness the novel is not devoid of humor, even about this theory. Religion may have changed, but Mrs. Swithin still wears a cross and annoys her brother by saying of the possibility of rain, "we can only pray." He, a modern skeptic, replies, "and provide umbrellas" (23). Isa recalls her dentist saying that "savages had false teeth" or perhaps that false teeth were first made during "the time of the pharoahs" (30). When Mrs. Swithin suggests that the same birds come yearly to the barn, the realistic Mrs. Manresa thinks "it was unlikely . . . that the birds were the same" (102).

The emotions which Isa thinks are universal are "Love. Hate. Peace." Both on stage and off, love and hate predominate, whether in thought or in interaction (Isa and Giles, Giles and Mrs. Manresa, Mr. Oliver and Isa, Mr. Oliver and his grandson . . .). Mrs. Manresa is attractive to men because she suggests a direct link to the sensual, productive life. Seeing her, Mr. Oliver "blessed the power of the human body to make the earth fruitful" (119). Such power makes Isa uncomfortable, even envious, and rouses "enmity" between her and her husband. To Miss La Trobe the pageant is a gift of love borne with much pain and some hatred. Waiting for a scene to begin, she "gnashed her teeth" and "crushed her manuscript" (122). Anger and pain are also aroused when she thinks the pageant fails since she "hadn't made them see." But when she can believe even for a moment that she has "made them see" (*even* "for one moment") she can rejoice in relief from torment (98). What she accomplishes then is to achieve peace for herself between the agony of creation and the agony of potential failure, and to give the audience a sense of unity which is likewise a source of peace. Before the play the audience is "too close, yet not close enough";

during the play Miss La Trobe judges that "she held them together" through great effort (98) and the audience does experience this, noting how "music makes us see the hidden, join the broken," hear the trees and birds "bid us . . . come together, crowd together" (120, cf. 160). At each interval the audience disperses, held loosely together by the continuous "tick, tick, tick" of the gramophone, like a clock reminding them of passing time. At the pageant's conclusion all are reluctant to separate, to return to the mundane from the world of strange mystery in which they have found peace (194 - 99). To the gramophone's usual announcement of a scene's end—"Dispersed are we; who have come together"—a line is now added: "Let us retain whatever made that harmony." And the audience echoes this desire, thinking (significantly in unison for the first time) "O let us . . . keep together. For there is joy, sweet joy, in company." It is disconcerting to descend to earth from the "golden glory" of what has earlier been described as a quasi-religious "festival" (76) taking place in a roofless church or "open-air cathedral" (65). Not all the members of the audience understand the pageant or are affected by it, though for some "the play hung in the sky of the mind" (212). But they have nonetheless been brought together for a moment of peace which is outside the chaos of their daily lives. As through the parties in *To the Lighthouse* and *The Waves*, or through Lily Briscoe's painting, by means of the pageant these characters have been shown the "message" of continuity, that life is not limited to the here and now.

Such feelings of unity and peace are brief. It is love and hate, the emotions Isa thinks dominate life, which dominate this novel. She may feel it is time for a new plot to be invented or for the author to emerge "from the bushes," but all that happens is that the butler arrives with the mail. After this, Isa and Giles are left alone for their final scene of love and hate (215 - 18). Although the novel occurs in peacetime, it is shadowed by war. Mrs. Swithin's inability to keep the prehistoric monsters of her book away from life in the present is echoed in Giles and Isa's son envisioning a dog as a "monster" on the attack (12). But real monsters roam the England of 1939 too, and sober-minded adults have reason for fear. In these last summer days before war was declared, even a peaceful English village could not ignore the airplanes whose roar interrupts the pageant. What "if the worst should come—let's hope it won't," they say and note that "things look worse than ever on the continent" (198 - 99). Giles is furious at his family's indifference to his "vision of Europe, bristling with guns, poised with planes. At any moment guns would rake that land into furrows," splintering the world he loved (53).

But the sources of war are nearer than the continent and less finite than a specific political party in a given country. The tension between love and hate is ever present, and individual "enmity" is not so very far removed from the national kind. It is much easier to describe or to accept a description of the distant Elizabethans or even the Victorians than to turn a mirror towards the Present Time. When the members of the audience are forced to see themselves in the pageant, "all shaded or evaded themselves." In spite of the flowers and birds, the world of the novel is not an attractive one; images of colors are matched by images of shadows. Unique to this novel among Virginia Woolf's works is the sheer volume of images of violence, disgust, or pain: blood-stained tennis shoes, prison bars, a snake choking on a toad dying in its mouth. The idea that people are not isolated from the natural world or from past and future but are part of a larger life may be designed theoretically to balance the bleakness which otherwise suffuses the book. To an audience increasingly certain that war is near, the thought that human life has at least survived centuries of periodic destructiveness may make the pageant a source of some comfort. But there is no telling for certain that this is the "meaning" of the pageant, for like a modernist novel, the pageant defies neat resolution. The novel as a whole reiterates the idea of life's continuity in the face of violence: the contemporary holders of the village names can look at the scars left by past military actions—Britons, Romans, Napoleon's troops. Perhaps then the coming generations will also have their chance to add to those scars, and their periods of peace between the violent acts of history.

Between the Acts is not a pleasant novel; the story it tells is too painful, its prognosis too negative, its scene too barren. The novel embodies some of the best of Virginia Woolf's abilities and some of her most notable defects. On the one hand there are abundant, varied, and evocative images, the clever parodies in the pageant (at least as interesting in what they tell about the history of English literature as *Orlando* is), and some unusually sympathetic characters. In fact, the novel reveals a greater awareness of the power of emotion than perhaps any of her novels and clothes this awareness in characters and situations that evoke rich response, even though the allegorical method, by removing so much realistic detail from the characters, might have precluded reader involvement. On the other hand, the language does suffer from the mixture of methods. The blend of prose and poetry in the intervals is especially jarring, and language use is not always consistent with the minds of those who use it. Virginia Woolf had begun another novel at the time of her death (to be called *Anon* and to be a "trip-through-English-Literature book"),[7] but *Between the Acts* has the feel of a last novel. It is hard to imagine Virginia Woolf writing a book with greater depth of understanding or more bleakness than this one.

CHAPTER 7

"Remember Ms. Woolf!"

A BOUT thirty years after Virginia Woolf's death, there was
a sudden increase of interest in her and in her writings. By the
end of the 1960's, Hogarth Press and Harcourt Brace (her British
and American publishers) had brought out new editions or reprints
of most of her books and had for the first time published the four
volumes of the "collected essays" and a fifth volume of reviews,
Contemporary Writers. Paperback editions of the short stories and
novels, *A Writer's Diary*, the essays, and the two feminist books also
appeared. Quentin Bell's two-volume biography, the first detailed
factual study of her life, was published in 1972. In the five years
between 1965 and 1969 just over fifty scholarly books and articles
about Virginia Woolf were published; in the next three years over
one hundred books and articles appeared. This trend seems to be
continuing. A journal devoted to Virginia Woolf and her circle
began publication in 1972; recent books and articles include
biographical studies, reminiscences, evaluations from psychological
and feminist stances, and analyses using quantitative methods
(computer-supported). Six volumes of her letters have begun to
appear in print. Autobiographical writings have been newly
published, and the complete diaries are being edited. What is
perhaps surprising about this renewed enthusiasm is that it is not
limited to the academic community. Bell's biography was a best
seller, bookstores report frequent sellouts of her works, especially *A
Room of One's Own*, *A Writer's Diary*, and some of the novels, and
articles about her appeared in *Ms.* and other popular magazines. A
little metal button like those used in political campaigns has been
seen in some feminist circles and on an occasional professor's
bulletin board defiantly asserting: "Remember Ms. Woolf!" Some
part of this heightened interest reflects the peaks of the hill and
valley terrain of reputation. Some results from interest feeding on
interest: excitement is generated by new information, published or

unpublished (Bell's biography, Leonard Woolf's autobiography, the increasing availability of the letters, diaries, and manuscripts). And some part is in response to the revival of a women's movement—hence a campaign button with "Ms." on it, a title Virginia Woolf is unlikely to have used, even if she could have known it.

Some of the reasons why Virginia Woolf is so attractive to feminists are readily apparent. She wrote two books about women (based on earlier lectures). Furthermore, in some ways her life can serve as a model of women's struggle for self-realization. In this process, Virginia Woolf was helped a great deal by Bloomsbury's attitudes towards homosexuality (and, simply, active sexuality), towards free thought in religion, and towards the roles of women and men within both family and society. But in spite of Bloomsbury, she experienced the pains of the modern feminist, being at odds with the social and sexual norms. And in spite of the many advantages of her birth, she experienced the frustrations of the intelligent woman striving for freedom in an age, a society, and a family unwilling to give it. When she talks in *A Room of One's Own* or *Three Guineas* about the necessities of an education, of guidance from parents, of encouragement from society, of cooperation from the woman's family, of privacy and freedom and time, Virginia Woolf could be talking about what she learned from her own experience.

Virginia Woolf's two books about women display a rhetorical stance aligned to feminism and tempered by facts. As she observes about *A Room of One's Own*, a "shrill feminine tone" in these books sometimes drowns out the quality of balanced good sense; she predicts in the same diary entry that this may appeal to some feminists but it is more likely to alienate other readers who will brush the studies aside or attack the author as a "feminist and . . . Sapphist" (AWD, 145). Even if they are propagandistic, the two books are more attractive than most polemic studies, because their author has a greater gift for language than most. In each book a semifictitious story adds unity and interest. When choosing examples to support a point Virginia Woolf considers appeal as well as documentary value. Scenes are described in sharp detail, with images which at times become symbols. For example, in *A Room of One's Own* she contrasts the richness of lunch at a men's college and the poverty of dinner at a women's college: a pudding at lunch is "a confection which rose all sugar from the waves," and is accom-

panied by rich and varied wines; at dinner the beef suggests "the
rumps of cattle in a muddy market . . . and women with string
bags on Monday morning," while water is served with the dry
biscuits and cheese which make up dessert. In the "glow" of the
first atmosphere good talk flourishes in a sense of comfortable good
will; in the second, conversation and talk of practical considerations
replace that of philosophy, the arts, or science (10 - 11, 17 - 18).
This is not mere propaganda but rather an artistry which suggests
that at least *A Room of One's Own* if not *Three Guineas* can outlast
its local interest.

I   A Room of One's Own

In 1928 Virginia Woolf was invited to lecture on "Women and
Fiction" at two British women's colleges, Newnham and Girton. *A
Room of One's Own*, a monograph expanded and revised from
those two talks, retains the spirit of a lecture, including direct
references to the audience and a refreshing casualness of language.
Although the essay is in fact to be read as a book, it displays some of
the colloquial structures more common to speech: phrases like "my
eye was caught" or "nobody cared a straw"; frequent intrusions by
the narrator—"But for women, I thought . . ." or "she will be a
poet, I said . . ."; tag-questions like "What were they blaming
Charlotte Brontë for, I wondered?"; and transitions between topics
(or even chapters) which are designed to sound spon-
taneous—"Happily my thoughts were now given another turn."
Within the guise of a lecture, a more involved fiction is developed,
as Virginia Woolf creates a person who acts out the process of
preparing to speak on the assigned topic. This character (who is to
be called Mary Beton, Mary Seton, Mary Carmichael, or any name
that pleases the reader) speaks for almost ninety percent of the
book, from a brief introduction to the conclusion where the author
summarizes in her own voice. "Mary Beton" is, of course, Virginia
Woolf, but the fiction makes possible a number of other fictions,
each of which functions thematically. For example, "Mary Beton"
visits Oxbridge (a concatenation of Oxford and Cambridge Univer-
sities) and Fernham (Girton and Newnham) on the same day, thus
heightening the effect of contrast between the men's and the
women's colleges. Other such fictions have "Mary" being chased
off the grass and denied entry to a library at Oxbridge because she
is a woman, while at Fernham she can hear the history of women's

colleges from a student, "Mary Seton"; and show her reading as a sample contemporary novel a fictitious work which is conveniently a composite of representative features.

The author's thesis is simply stated but she develops it carefully in the book: certain conditions are most conducive to success as a writer, and these conditions have not, until relatively recent times, been available for women. Like so much else in the book, its title is symbolic. "A room of one's own" suggests privacy and perhaps time to write, freedom to choose a career, "the power to think for oneself" (110). It implies also a certain level of financial independence (defined as about 500 pounds a year) which in turn stands for freedom from the unrewarding labor which makes writing a desired avocation rather than an active vocation. Money also makes education available, and education (knowledge of the classics and other literature as well as the experience which such contact may confer) is essential not only for a writer but also for full development of human potential. A tradition of women professionals, whatever the field, is necessary to force changes in society's attitudes toward women's roles. Few women will become writers or doctors, inventors or politicians if they must battle parents who scoff at their professional plans, a society which expects them in their teens to accept husbands chosen for them and then to give birth to a large number of children, even (in modern times) parents and teachers who do not encourage them to explore whatever areas appeal to them. A room of one's own, money, education, a corps of women professionals, and a tradition of women authors are the items which Virginia Woolf believes necessary to create the best state of mind possible for a woman to become a writer. In the essay these arguments unfold gradually, supported by various kinds of evidence (historical, political, and literary) and often made more palatable by the author's creative imagination.

In Chapter One, having lunched richly at Oxbridge and dined poorly at Fernham, "Mary Beton" contrasts the wealth which has for centuries endowed the archetypal men's school with the struggle for subsistence funds which less than a century earlier led to the founding of the first English college for women. In the nineteenth century the idea that women should be educated (or, for that matter, *could* be educated) was startling; until late in the century women did not own property and therefore had little incentive to work, even if they could find acceptable jobs or had time between pregnancies. She notes that "making a fortune and bearing thirteen

children" is a hopeless combination (22). The restrictions built of tradition might be stifling at Oxbridge, but men at least had access to a liberal education long before women. "Mary" regrets that the newer women's colleges cannot yet compete in academic experience or in the atmosphere which fosters free thought.

In Chapter Two "Mary Beton" turns to the social scientists and philosophers to learn why women are poor. This one question soon generates fifty more, each with many conflicting answers. She is overwhelmed by the sheer numbers of books about women, initially piqued to see how many are by people with no special qualifications, and later seriously disturbed by the worthlessness of most. Written in passion (and usually by men), the books reveal an anger which makes them untrustworthy. Exploring the source of this emotion, she theorizes that for both men and women, life is "a perpetual struggle" requiring "gigantic courage and strength" and especially a self-confidence which might be generated by denigrating other people. Hence, women have for years served as "looking-glasses possessing the magic and delicious power of reflecting the figure of man at twice its natural size." This may help explain why women are necessary and, she concludes, why a woman's criticism so hurts and angers a man (35 - 36). Such analysis and later speculations about how history would differ if women had not assumed this role reveal that "Mary" (i.e., Virginia Woolf) can also speak from "emotion" rather than "truth"; here, because the emotion is not anger, the tone is not strident, but emotion has nonetheless led reason astray. "Mary Beton" ends this survey of women in history by observing how even in her lifetime opportunities have increased for the woman who wants to work or participate in government while the possibility of financial independence has grown, and she predicts that further developments will ultimately affect every aspect of woman's life, from her interests to her self-valuation to her lifespan.

Noting that women play more varied roles in literature than historical fact would lead one to suspect, "Mary Beton" suggests that there is a need to "re-write history," taking into account the "average" woman about whom far too little is known (47). From the limited available data she fabricates a model of what life would have been like for a woman writer in Elizabethan England, in order to determine what conditions best foster writing. Suppose Shakespeare had a talented sister, she asks, what would have happened to her? The answer is perhaps predictable but the author

clothes it in lively detail. "Judith Shakespeare" is not sent to school, taught to read Latin, or given books; if she chances upon a book her parents tell her to do her mending or stir the soup pot. They speak with firm kindness because they know what life is really like for a woman. Threatened with marriage against her wishes, wanting to avoid conflict with her parents, and above all hoping to become a writer, Judith runs away to London, where the men at the theaters first laugh at her naïvete (women cannot act, women cannot write) and later take advantage of it. Unmarried, pregnant, and desolate, Judith commits suicide. This story makes several points: a woman like Judith had no chance to develop her talent. Even if she braved the odds against her she still had to find the courage to deal with the resultant "inner struggle . . . all the conditions of her life, all her own instincts, were hostile to the state of mind which is needed to set free whatever is in the brain." From this conclusion, Virginia Woolf can have "Mary Beton" slide easily into a consideration of "the state of mind that is most propitious to the act of creation" (52). This state of mind results from the conditions enumerated earlier: financial security, peace, freedom, encouragement—all symbolized by that private room. Such conditions may lead to the best writing, where the author's mind is "unimpeded" by the worries or ill will which external pressures can cause (58 - 59).

In the next chapter the narrator uses a brief history of women in literature to uncover the gradual development of an appropriate "state of mind" in women writers. Books written out of anger will be "disfigured and deformed" she argues (64), as the antagonism frequent in the few extant works by women from before 1800 shows. Until women could earn money by writing, even they tended to look down on their activity, but "money dignifies what is frivolous if unpaid for" (68). Until the twentieth century women tended to write novels, perhaps because novel writing suited the way they lived. "Mary Beton" suggests that since novels require "less concentration" than poems or plays, they can be written in the family living room during rare periods of free time. Further, novels tend to be about human relations, supposedly of special interest to women; tradition and experience limited women to relatively few topics. England is a patriarchy, "Mary Beton" argues, in which "masculine values . . . prevail" (77). This makes it difficult for a woman's interests to be considered significant or for a woman to assert her freedom from the received values. In describing another barrier faced by the fledgling woman author, Virginia Woolf

(through her speaker) walks on untested ground, for she assumes that women write differently from men, whether in forming sentences or in using a given genre. She even becomes prescriptive, though she hedges the prescription with both tentativeness and an appeal to objectivity: "At a venture one would say that women's books should be shorter, more concentrated, than those of men," for rarely will a woman find long periods of uninterrupted time (81). Considering that she earlier argues that once women's roles start to change it is reasonable to suppose that any aspect of life may be affected, it may be fallacious to assume role differences will persist. Virginia Woolf, through her persona, is guilty of faults earlier ascribed to those angry, unscientific writers whose books on women are catalogued in libraries.

The modern woman writer selects from a wide range of topics and genres, for she has advanced far enough to see that writing is an art, not only a means of "self-expression" (83). In this fifth chapter "Mary Beton" pretends to read a novel published "this very month" (84) in order to make tangible her comments about modern female authors. While not a work of genius, the imaginary novel interests her because it describes women in roles other than relationships with men. No longer wasting energy in pent-up anger against men, the fictitious novelist reveals her "fear and hatred" only by a "slight exaggeration of the joy of freedom, a tendency to the caustic and satirical" in discussing men (96). Because of these encouraging signs "Mary Beton" can exclaim that given "another hundred years," a room of her own, and an independent income, such a novelist will be "a poet" (98).

In the final chapter Virginia Woolf offers something of an antidote to the sexual one-sidedness of the essay so far. Aware of the satisfaction she derives from watching a man and a woman walk together, "Mary Beton" wonders whether like the body, the mind had two sexes which strive for union and balance. She postulates that in the "normal and comfortable state," the state most conducive to creativity, the male and female aspects of the mind "live in harmony" (102). The fusion of two balanced elements is what Virginia Woolf refers to when she describes "the androgynous mind," whether here or in such works as *Orlando* and *The Waves*. In *A Room of One's Own* she argues through her persona that "the androgynous mind" shows less concern with distinctions between the masculine and feminine and can thus avoid the strident sex consciousness which perverts much modern literature. In continuing

this argument Virginia Woolf again steps onto the unstable ground
of speculation: literature written by an author who lacks even "a
spark of the woman" is "crude and immature," lacks "suggestive
power," and has no appeal for women (106); such literature
depends on the "masculine" quality of intellect, so that "the other
faculties of the mind harden and become barren." She pronounces
Shakespeare, Keats, and Sterne to be androgynous authors, saying
that Proust may have too much of the female in him while Milton,
Wordsworth, and Tolstoi have too much of the male (107).

In the concluding pages of the essay Virginia Woolf retires the
fiction of "Mary Beton" preparing a lecture and addresses her
audience directly. She refuses to judge men and women comparatively even as authors because all such "measurement" is
"futile" (110); (she would have been wise to consider further the
danger of such comparisons as she had already made). She justifies
her emphasis on "material things" both by explaining the symbolism inherent in a private room or five hundred pounds a year
and by quoting the opinion of a respected academic authority, that
the poor have virtually no hope of obtaining the education or
" 'intellectual freedom of which great writings are born.' " And, she
continues in her own words, "intellectual freedom depends upon
material things. Poetry depends upon intellectual freedom. And
women have always been poor" (111 - 12). But now, because of the
efforts of many women in the past and, oddly, because of two wars
(the Crimean War and World War I), the situation is changing for
the better. New colleges and new job opportunities have opened,
women can vote and own property, they have more free time
because they have fewer children. Thus her audience can strive
with a reasonable chance of success for the conditions which make
"great writings" possible. Even if no one in the audience should
write a noteworthy book, still the writer lives an "invigorating" life,
more consciously in touch with "reality": so she explains that
writing has value for the individual and potentially for all people
(113 - 16). In an aside during her final exhortation, Virginia Woolf
reiterates an idea frequently present in her fiction but never so
direct as here—that there is a continuous human community: "My
belief is that if we live another century or so—I am talking of the
common life which is the real life and not of the little separate lives
which we live as individuals—and have five hundred a year each of
us and rooms of our own; if we have the habit of freedom and the
courage to write exactly what we think; if we . . . see human beings

not always in their relation to each other but in relation to reality"
then all the dead "sisters" of great male writers will be reborn. But
Judith Shakespeare can flourish only if "we" prepare the way for
her (117 - 18). This upbeat if also admonitory conclusion differs
from Virginia Woolf's private description of her lecture at Girton.
Privately she stresses the difficulties facing those "starved," brave,
intelligent, poor women, eager to learn and experience but "destin-
ed to become schoolmistresses." Yet even though she mocks her in-
delicacy in "blandly" telling them to have their own rooms and to
drink wine instead of water, and in a pique describes them as
"egotistical" and inadequately "impressed by [her] age and
repute," still she repeats the faith that upholds the essay: "I fancy
sometimes the world changes. I think I see reason spreading"
(AWD, 131 - 32).

II   Three Guineas

   Within a year or two of publishing her first book about women,
Virginia Woolf began to think of a new book, a sequel she calls
variously "Professions for Women," "Opening the Door," and "my
war book" (AWD, 161 - 62, 253). For years schemes for the sequel
are fleetingly mentioned, but not until 1938 was *Three Guineas*
published. *The Times* acclaimed it as "a call to women" (AWD,
285), other reviewers attacked it with equal force (see 288, 290,
315), and Virginia Woolf described it as "the mildest childbirth I
have ever had" (284). Each of these responses makes sense. The
book is assuredly a "call to women," with specific recommendations. Without being violent it is opinionated, which explains the
attacks. Although *Three Guineas* required more extensive research
than any of Virginia Woolf's other books, its emotional demands
upon its author seem less. If *Three Guineas* resulted from Virginia
Woolf's "mildest childbirth" it is perhaps because the book is a kind
of stepchild. It did not take life from that inmost self which at times
in her career was drained by the tension of creative writing, nor is it
about those things that mattered most to its author. Virginia
Woolf's genius lies in the delicacy of analysis, not in persuasion, and
her interest in feminism while genuine is nonetheless peripheral.
Like *A Room of One's Own*, *Three Guineas* represents good tract
writing, but for all its mastery it is propaganda, not the kind of art
its author could produce.
   Virginia Woolf adopts a fictive pose in *Three Guineas* not only to

give it unity but also to make it seem that she was invited to write the book.[1] In each of the three chapters the narrator (who is differentiated from the author only by the fiction of letter writing) pretends to be responding to a request for support from the "honorary treasurers" of fundraising drives for buildings at a women's college, for an organization of educated women seeking employment in the professions, and for a society to prevent war and protect "culture and intellectual liberty." In opening she begins a letter to the third writer but explains that to answer him she must also respond to the others: the three causes are "the same and inseparable" (144). This treasurer's pro forma question—how can war be prevented (and implicitly, will she join his society's efforts to prevent war)—is taken seriously by the narrator, who transforms the passive question into a series of active ones: what influence can she, a woman, have? how can she act? why should her correspondent expect that she or any group of women would be able to affect the course of history? It is in attempting to describe these problems that the narrator turns to the other letters requesting support, to explain that women and men differ fundamentally in their training and therefore their values, in their opportunities and therefore their influence. Until he sees these differences he cannot hope to understand her eventual answer to his question. Thus he must learn something of the history of women in England, particularly their economic conditions and their education (either paid and formal or unpaid and informal) which molds them through parents, society, and tradition.

Women have no firsthand experience of war, the narrator explains; more importantly their training has not traditionally given them sympathy with the reasons why men go to war. Why should women feel loyal to a given country when they must adopt their husband's nationality upon marriage? Why would they wish to defend the land of a country when they have no right to own property? Without necessarily being angered by such conditions, they feel indifference about the usual causes of war. Yet men and women react with like horror when confronted with the brutal effects of battles. Thus she finds his three suggestions (sign a public letter, join his society, contribute money) inadequate, however laudable. Direct action through the armed service or Stock Exchange is impossible, she argues, because these are closed to women; the diplomatic service and church are virtually closed too. Women's influence is at best indirect: traditionally they have manipulated personal influence; "today" they can vote, express their opinions more freely, and use their limited money to affect those with greater power. In time women may be able to make changes in society which will undercut the urge to battle. For example, they can support education designed to instill hatred of war. She argues that so far education has not taught this to people; university-educated men fought partisan battles against colleges for women—a possessiveness historically associated with war. So, she suggests, women must change education to fit the new ideals. Thus she considers next the letter from a women's college building fund, concluding that she will donate to the fund only if her guinea will be used to help develop a society opposed to war. She recognizes that colleges must train students for careers, but suggests they also should emphasize the fine and humane arts, and especially the art of communication, rather than the arts of domination and war. Furthermore, jobs bring money which provides independence which in turn provides influence. The most traditional education, if it gives women the chance to find professions besides marriage, opens new doors. So long as marriage is a woman's only career she will be tempted to preserve the status quo, including those loyalties of property and family which lead to war. Having reached this conclusion, the narrator sends off her first guinea in support of education for women.

The narrator's argument so far, however one-sided, has at least this merit: that historically there have always been wars in England and that the role of women changed dramatically in the preceding century. As Virginia Woolf argues in *A Room of One's Own*, if that role changes enough, there is no way to predict what will be affected; already there were masses of women capable of direct, influential action. Besides, it is obviously possible to favor increased education for women in accord with the less flamboyant theses advanced here. For instance, women should be allowed to develop their potential and encouraged to contribute to society in various ways, not only through a family. In the second chapter, Virginia Woolf extends this argument to suggest that important as the *professions* of wife and mother are, they are only two of the many which a woman may engage in. Because independence of thought and action operates best when the actor is free from external constraints, it may be related to financial independence. Thus, she argues, support of education for women should be accompanied by aid in obtaining suitable paid employment. Examining the reasons why women cannot find jobs or adequate pay, she finds that the primary cause has roots in primitive emotions: fearing change, people continue patterns which are comfortable precisely because they are habitual—women work in the home, men support women and children. Fear may also underlie such contentions as that women disrupt offices or that women cannot work as well as men. She uses statistics which display disparities in men's and women's salaries to argue that women are underpaid by the public for their "public service." Their "private service" as wives and mothers is unsalaried: they receive nothing from public funds and have no necessary share in their husband's income after living expenses common to both are deducted (57). The writer makes two connections between this situation and the question about preventing war, one more subtle and inflammatory than the other. When English society tries to tell women through direct comments (quoted from various sources) or through prejudicial treatment that their place is in the home or that they are inferior to men, this society is as tyrannical as any enemy government: until the "Dictator" at home is crushed, it is unfair to expect women to help "crush him abroad" (53). The narrator's second argument cannot arouse the the kind of objection which the first is likely to: since married women are unpaid and working women are underpaid it is fruitless to ask the first for donations and unfair to ask the second. Nonetheless, the second must be asked. With this reasoning the narrator agrees to donate to the society if it promises that professions will be practiced so as to encourage women's participation and to prevent future wars. Furthermore, working women must avoid becoming so enmeshed in either the hours or the competition that they lose interest in the family or culture. Only a "civilized human being," she argues, can hope to prevent war by maintaining an appropriate hierarchy of values. To become fully productive members of their society and yet remain "civilized," women might rely on their unique unpaid education, combining its special virtues with the wealth, knowledge, and power newly available. The old "teachers" to be retained are poverty (not striving for unnecessary money), mental chastity (refusing to adulterate one's work for money), derision (rejecting honors and self-advertisements), and "freedom from unreal loyalties" such as pride in one's country, religion, school, sex, or family (78 - 80).

Having discussed ways women might obtain the education and jobs giving them influence, the narrator can turn in the last chapter directly to the first request for funds. Women must attempt to preserve culture and freedom of thought, the two conditions which her correspondent says are necessary if war is to be avoided. The narrator readily agrees to give her third guinea to this cause and to do so freely, without any of the conditions she imposed on the other two gifts. She cannot doubt that the writer's aims are hers: to prevent war by supporting personal freedom, democracy, and the ideal of equal opportunity. With this new unity of aims between men and women, she contends that there is no longer a use for the word "feminist," because now the fight against tyranny is not limited to one sex.

Although she gladly donates to her correspondent's cause, the narrator will not take the second step he requests, of joining his society. It is not enough for women to fight against war by refusing to join the armed services (which do not welcome them anyway) or by failing to make munitions or act as nurses in wartime, or even by discouraging men's interest in war. They must acknowledge that they are a "Society of Outsiders" which may share the aims of the society to which she has been invited but which attempts to reach them by means derived from a set of values dependent upon a different sex, tradition, and education (113). Women are bucking centuries of male dominance, but they are changing their lives. The premise of her argument is that "the public and private worlds are inseparably connected" (142): change in one is not possible without change in the other. Thus, she concludes, it was not possible to respond to the request from the pacifist society without also responding to the other two requests; it is not possible to answer in isolation the fundamental question of how to prevent war.

In *Three Guineas* Virginia Woolf's argument at times cannot be sustained. For example, she asserts that the tyrant against whom the nineteenth-century feminists struggled was no different from the new tyrant, Fascism, or its embodiments, Hitler and Mussolini (101 - 102). Her zeal leads her to such unfounded assertions and comparisons which (however attractive they may be to zealots) are rash. In spite of such flaws, the books is basically well assembled, careful in its structure, and often reasonable, even creative, in its recommendations. It includes a spirited factual account of the causes and history of the women's movement in England. Nearly forty years later some of her observations might still be considered noteworthy by feminists, for that word has not been retired, as Virginia Woolf had hoped. The valid observations include noting the inconsistency that when convenient for society (as in World War

I) women suddenly are found capable of simultaneously working and raising children, but when this is inconvenient (as in times of high unemployment) the idea that motherhood is a full-time occupation is elevated to an ideal, and suggesting that childrearing should not necessarily be only the woman's responsibility or privilege (139 - 41). *Three Guineas* lacks the charm of *A Room of One's Own*, although at times it reveals Virginia Woolf's sharpness of analysis and unique use of language. In one section which combines wit with imagination, she describes the uniforms symbolizing a hierarchy of what some consider merit—those distinctions of costume which "advertise the social, professional, or intellectual standing of the wearer." Addressing the men who affect such distinctions, the narrator continues: "If you will excuse the humble illustration, your dress fulfills the same function as the tickets in a grocer's shop. But, here, instead of saying, 'This is margarine; this pure butter; this is the finest butter in the market,' it says, 'This man is a clever man—he is Master of Arts; this man is a very clever man—he is Doctor of Letters; this man is a most clever man—he is a Member of the Order of Merit' " (20). This, the reader may wish to say, shows a good writer straining just slightly too hard to be clever herself. Still, passages like this remind the reader that after all Virginia Woolf's strength lies in creative writing, not in such propaganda as *Three Guineas* (or *A Room of One's Own*), however much the "causes" may have moved her.

III   *Conclusion*

A few feminists inhabit the world of Virginia Woolf's novels—Mary Dachet, for example, in *Night and Day*. There are also women scientists like Peggy Pargiter as well as traditional women (like Eleanor Pargiter or Mrs. Ramsay) whose lives are oriented about their families. The men and women in her novels function as students, hostesses, professionals, dilettantes, travellers, stay-at-homes, farmers, city dwellers, diplomats, and even laborers, though admittedly the population of her world is primarily upper-middle class. Perhaps the most dominant category, however, is that of artists, usually dissatisfied artists. For some, like Rachel Vinrace, frustration results when she needs to hide a commitment to the arts from unsympathetic companions, who may in turn represent a world uninterested in or even secretly afraid of art. Nearly all the artists struggle to create. That it takes Orlando four centuries to write one poem she can take pride in is obvious exaggeration, but Lily Briscoe (who works ten years on variants of one picture until she is satisfied) constantly fears that she is inadequate and even that her style is unfashionable. (An art instructor visiting a few years earlier had taught all the amateur artists in the area to use the same pale shades of pink and lemon.) Even those artists who, like Lily, successfully complete a painting, or like Miss La Trobe, produce a play, suffer when their work is not understood, because art provides two values to its creator—the relief of expressing a vision and the possibility of communicating that vision to another person. Since for these artists (and their creator) art is a form of communication, the failure in interpersonal relations of Neville and Mr. Carmichael, the only commercially successful poets Virginia Woolf describes, takes on poignant significance. Not that her artists despair alone in metaphorically locked rooms. Lily paints her picture, for once capturing graphically what she sees; Miss La Trobe's play affects some members of her audience; Rachel Vinrace plays the piano for Terence Hewet as he daydreams about his novel. But Rachel dies and it is unlikely that Terence will write a novel. In his summary (his supreme creative achievement) Bernard says that the book of notes for his long-planned novel has dropped to the floor to be swept away like so much dust.

Are these cases of inadequacy? Does the failure lie in the artist or in his world? Bernard, probably Virginia Woolf's most direct spokesperson, at last learns to distrust art's tendency to order reality and thus perhaps to falsify it. But he has another fear too, that his notebook may be filled with "shadows." The question he implicitly asks is as basic to Virginia Woolf's world view as any to be asked: what is the correspondence between the truth (the world, reality, nature) and the individual's perception? Various characters at various times sense chaos or stability, the ridiculous posturing of ceremony or the comfort of tradition in ritual, the joy of birth or its sorrow, the pain of death or its release; they see people as brutal or suffering, bestial or holy; they fear solitude or rejoice in its freeing them from constraint. The very "sense of the complexity and the reality and the struggle" (*The Waves*, 381) may be a reminder of how intensely one can live. This variety simply reiterates the complex nature of life, both the objective facts (that death can be a tragedy or a relief, that the same person can by turns be tender or abrupt) and the subjective interpretations of those facts (that the same act may be perceived now as kindness, later as cruelty). At the center of existence, as Bernard says, lies not an answer but a shadow holding perhaps "something," perhaps "nothing"; neither he nor his creator can "know."

Virginia Woolf explores questions in her fiction that remain essentially unchanged and always important to every generation of novel readers. She asks what might be the significance of the most basic experiences (birth and death, for instance), relationships (being a parent or child, friend or lover), and feelings (anger, shame, love, hate, peace). She wants to know what the relationship between the actual event or situation and any available perceptions of it may be. And she suggests through the discrepancies between one character's ideas about himself or another individual and the ideas of a second character, or through the disparity between the actual size of a pool or the measured elapsed time of an action and the various interpretations of these objective data that there is, in fact, only a limited correspondence between perception and reality. People's understanding of life is not especially accurate. The answers to those traditional questions of literature—if anyone dare to suggest answers—cannot be the same as they once were. About the value of the most basic experiences, as about perception itself, there is doubt.

The optimism with which Bloomsbury began did not last even the lifetime of its early participants. The masses were not interested in art, the League of Nations did not ensure peace, obtaining the vote did not raise women to equal standing with men, one world war was followed by a second. In this modern world no grail is found at the end of the journey, for uncertainty is the keynote and potential answers are replaced by the "central shadow," an "inscrutable" shadow. Love and friendship, those Bloomsbury ideals, might not last and could bring pain. Taking over where human intercourse failed, art could not break through the barriers between people or surmount them to lead people to a world of eternal inner peace. The new religion—faith in people led by the priests of art—proved no more an absolute than those earlier rejected ones. But the fact that art fails to offer absolute solace does not make it worthless, just as the fact that no one finds a grail does not rob the journey of value. After all, there are adventures to be experienced along the way. The costs of painting a picture or writing a poem are many—energy, dedication, pain, anger—but so are the rewards when for once the artist's vision is expressed, perhaps even shared. The effort of communicating with another person or of creating the opportunity for a moment of unity among friends is likewise great, but success provides the joy that is relief from loneliness. Having seen the horror under the surface Virginia Woolf sought to cover it over with her own kind of order. For a time she succeeded but by the final works the cover seemed to be slipping off. *Three Guineas* stridently proclaims a path to a better world but its very stridency reveals her lack of faith; *Between the Acts* is permeated with violence, barren with despair. She could not exorcise "the central shadow" nor could she decorate around it, like her own Mrs. Dalloway and Mrs. Ramsay. Hers is a highly personal vision with roots deep in her psyche, but it is also representative. She is not alone in her search for a new order, a new set of answers to replace those previously found by means of traditional religion, values, and knowledge. This search and its failure create the modernists' quasi-religious dilemma. Like many twentieth-century writers, Virginia Woolf finally attempts to find the necessary order in art. Her writings are difficult because of this, and because (as she says in condemning George Meredith's novels) in successful fiction like hers the "philosophy" is "consumed" or made an intrinsic part of plot and character, so that it cannot be extracted in easily remembered phrases.[2] But that, of course, is because she *is* an artist.

Virginia Woolf confronts and denies romantic conceptions of the possibility of art as she confronts and denies traditional inter-pretations of reality and human identity or literary character and plot structure. Her exploration of ideas has its limits, as does the world of her novels (in scope) or the presentation of that world (in tangible detail). She is not a philosopher after all, but an artist, determined not to present a codified interpretation of reality but creatively to shape some aspects of a constantly shifting personal perception of that reality. That she omits from her novels the coal miners of D. H. Lawrence's fiction or the tavern-goers of James Joyce's matters less than what she includes and how she transforms the people and problems she does include into art. We will not forget "Ms. Woolf" because her characters are from one social stratum, her aesthetic theory lacks unity, and her feminist tracts are propagandistic. Rather, we will remember Virginia Woolf because at her best she can challenge us with intricate patterns of language and action, delight us with her sympathetic understanding of peo-ple, and charm us by the beauty of her language or the surprise of an unexpected image. She can invite us into another world, super-ficially very different from our "here and now" but recognizably a real reflection of something we know as life.

Notes and References

Chapter One

1. "Hugh Selwyn Mauberley," in *Personae* (New York: New Directions, 1962), pp. 190 - 91.

2. The standard biography is Quentin Bell, *Virginia Woolf* (New York: Harcourt Brace Jovanovich, 1972). Supplementary information can be found in *The Letters of Virginia Woolf, The Diary of Virginia Woolf* (and its excerpts in *A Writer's Diary*), *Moments of Being,* Aileen Pippett, *The Moth and the Star: A Biography of Virginia Woolf* (Boston: Little, Brown, 1955) and in Joan Russell Noble, *Recollections of Virginia Woolf* (New York: William Morrow, 1972). The volumes of Leonard Woolf's autobiography covering the years 1911 to 1969 offer comments of a personal and yet surprisingly objective nature about his wife's personality, habits, talents, and illnesses. Nigel Nicolson discusses the relationship between his mother (Vita Sackville-West) and Virginia Woolf in *Portrait of a Marriage: V. Sackville-West and Harold Nicolson* (New York: Atheneum, 1973).

3. Two stories from the *Hyde Park Gate News* have been published in Woolf's *A Cockney's Farming Experiences.*

4. See Bell, I, 42 - 44 and "About Gerald Duckworth," *Virginia Woolf Miscellany,* 6 (1977); and Virginia Woolf, "A Sketch of the Past," *Moments of Being.*

5. In discussing this suicide attempt, Quentin Bell notes that he finds no proof that Virginia first tried to kill herself in 1895, after her mother's death, as others have suggested (I, 90). Leonard Woolf speaks of Virginia's attempt to kill herself "by jumping out of a window" in 1895; see *Beginning Again,* p. 77.

6. J.K. Johnstone offers a comprehensive examination of Bloomsbury and of Virginia Woolf's involvement in that society in *The Bloomsbury Group* (New York: Noonday, 1954). See also Quentin Bell, *Bloomsbury* (London: Weidenfeld and Nicolson, 1968) and David Gadd, *The Loving Friends* (London: The Hogarth Press, 1974). E. M. Forster's novel, *Howards End,* is in part a fictionalized view of the Stephen sisters, especially during the main Bloomsbury period. Margaret Schlegel's vision of life, her attempt to sort out the values of art and personal relationships, even her hesitations, social attitudes, and impracticalities reflect aspects of Virginia.

7. See especially *Beginning Again,* 75 - 82 and 149 - 64. The quotations which follow are from these pages.

8. See Joan Russell Noble, *Recollections of Virginia Woolf* (New York: William Morrow, 1972). The focus of this collection of essays, assessments, and anecdotes is on Virginia Woolf's personality and personal habits, but it includes her writing, madness, marriage, and the time and society in which she lived.

9. "My thoughts turn well up, to write the first chapter of the next book (nameless) Anon, it will be called" (AWD, 345).

10. The letter is quoted in Bell, II, 226.

Chapter Two

1. This is a frequently repeated idea in Virginia Woolf's writings and will be discussed in connection with characterization in the novels. One example is this: "I see that there are four? dimensions: all to be produced, in human life . . . I mean: I; and the not I; and the outer and the inner—no I'm too tired to say: but I see it" (AWD, 250).

2. CE II, 275; CE I, 263 - 64, 298; AWD, 236. She objects, for example, to the strident sex-consciousness which has sometimes marred the writings of women and more recently (she observes) that of the men who are responding to the challenges of the women's movement (*Room*, 102 - 108; cf. CE II, 144).

3. She is happy to have found "some idea of a new form for a new novel. . . . What the unity shall be I have yet to discover; the theme is a blank to me; but I see immense possibilities in the form I hit upon . . ." (AWD, 22; cf. 276). One reason for her excitement about form is that some new "method" may bring "fresh subjects in view, because I saw the chance of being able to say them" (AWD, 101).

4. Cf. AWD, 203: "Form then, is the sense that one thing follows another rightly."

5. E. M. Forster wrote or spoke about Woolf's work as a novelist and a critic in several places, including "A New Novelist" in "*Albergo Empedocle*" *and Other Writings*, ed. George H. Thomson (New York: Liveright, 1971), "The Early Novels of Virginia Woolf," *Abinger Harvest* (New York: Harcourt, Brace and World, 1936), and the 1941 Rede lecture, "Virginia Woolf." These were all part of a continuing dialogue between the two, both novelists and critics, antagonists and friends.

Chapter Three

1. The collection *A Haunted House and Other Short Stories* contains all but two of the stories originally published in *Monday or Tuesday* (1921), which itself included the separately printed *Kew Gardens* (1919), as well as a selection of stories published in various magazines between 1922 and 1941 and several unpublished pieces. According to the "Foreword" to the volume, Leonard Woolf's purpose was to fulfill his wife's desire to publish such a collection, and he attempted to make the selections she would have

made. This volume (in which appear all the stories mentioned in the text) is thus widely representative of Virginia Woolf's achievements in the genre.
 2. The bibliography of Woolf criticism in *Modern Fiction Studies* (Autumn 1972) lists articles and sections of books on the collection *A Haunted House* and on specific stories.
 3. The analysis of emotion was obviously of great interest to the Bloomsbury Group. It is worth noting too the date of the author's marriage, and easy to imagine such conversations occurring between Virginia Stephen and Leonard Woolf in 1911 or 1912 when this novel was being written.
 4. A child-mother element enters into many of Virginia Woolf's relationships with other women, whether Violet Dickinson, Vita Sackville-West, or Woolf's own sister, Vanessa Bell. Her letters especially suggest that she seemed attracted to maternal warmth and strength rather than sexuality in the women she loved, and she addresses them more in the words of a child than a lover.
 5. Compare in *To the Lighthouse* Mrs. Ramsay's insistence on the importance of marriage (though hardly its ease) for men and women alike.

Chapter Four

 1. See "Phases of Fiction," "Modern Fiction," and "Mr. Bennett and Mrs. Brown," all in *Collected Essays*.
 2. When Thoby Stephen went up to Cambridge in 1899, he was Jacob's age. Also, like Jacob, he travelled in Greece, and 1906 is significant in being the year he died (at twenty-six, thus again—as near as the reader can tell—like Jacob).
 3. See also Chapter 2 above, especially Section IV.
 4. For example, this is a description of Jacob's books: "There were books enough; very few French books; but then anyone who's worth anything reads just what he likes, as the mood takes him, with extravagant enthusiasm" (39). This could be the narrator's comment but is more likely to be a defensive remark Jacob would make to himself or to a student like Bonamy whose knowledge of French lets him enjoy books Jacob cannot read. In this instance Jacob's feelings (mainly of inadequacy) are eventually revealed, thus offering further support for the hypothesis that the boundaries between the omniscient narrator and Jacob's point of view are slippery. A similar example of shifts in point of view can be found in the effusion about letter writing (92 - 94).
 5. Virginia Woolf paraphrases her American publisher (Harcourt Brace): "'We think *Jacob's Room*· an extraordinarily distinguished and beautiful work. You have, of course, your own method, and it is not easy to foretell how many readers it will have; surely it will have enthusiastic ones, and we delight in publishing it'" (AWD, 50).
 6. This notion is especially significant in *The Waves* (see Chapter 5) and is prominent also in *Flush* (see Section IV, below), but it appears in

many of the other novels. For example, in *The Years*, as Peggy Pargiter shares a cab with her Aunt Eleanor, she wonders if they are really two separate people, and asks, "Where does she begin, and where do I end?" (334). Likewise Eleanor notes "my life's been other people's lives," and she lists her father, her friends, and ends with Nicholas, a specific friend. As if to prove the mystical reality of her belief, even as Eleanor thinks of him Nicholas appears, accompanied by the observation "it was like . . . a part of her, coming to the surface" (367 - 68). In *To The Lighthouse*, this idea is metaphorically expressed in two juxtaposed scenes. After Lily cries out in vain for the dead Mrs. Ramsay, the scene shifts to the boat in which Mr. Ramsay, Cam, and James are making their penitential pilgrimage to the Lighthouse. There "Macalister's boy" cuts a chunk from a fish caught for bait: "The mutilated body (it was alive still) was thrown back into the sea." Immediately the scene reverts to Lily, still hopelessly crying (268 - 69). Like the fish, Lily is alive though mutilated, having lost a part of herself through the death of Mrs. Ramsay.

7. Specific parallels between Septimus and his creator abound. Especially striking are the birds singing in Greek (35 - 36, cf. Bell, I, 90). Clarissa Dalloway's attitude toward sex also seems similar to Virginia Woolf's.

8. Alex Page, "A Dangerous Day: Mrs. Dalloway Discovers Her Double," *Modern Fiction Studies*, CE II (1961), 123. Of the many essays on this subject, Nathalia Wright suggests that Mrs. Dalloway's postulated reasons for suicide are Septimus's problems, including "the pressure exerted upon the soul by passionless men." See "*Mrs. Dalloway*: A Study in Composition," *College English*, V, vii (1944), 351 - 52. Keith Hollingsworth develops the Freudian interpretation, finding in Septimus and Clarissa respectively the death and life instincts of one individual; see "Freud and the Riddle of *Mrs. Dalloway*," in *Studies in Honor of John Wilcox* (Detroit, 1958), pp. 239 - 49. Anna S. Benjamin notes that Smith was born in the year Clarissa rejects Peter's proposal and that Clarissa, having "died" then, is not reborn until the night of Smith's suicide. See "Towards an Understanding of the Meaning of Virginia Woolf's *Mrs. Dalloway*," *Wisc Studs in Cont Lit*, VI (1965), 220 - 21.

9. Clarissa defends herself against attacks by comparing her parties with Richard's Parliamentary work for some groups she cannot recall. Parties are "her gift," that is her talent and also "an offering." Doris Kilman's aspersion on this view cannot be taken as Virginia Woolf's disapproval, for Miss Kilman's bitterness makes it impossible for her to live up to her ideal (perhaps her pose) as "Christian" (182 - 90).

10. Because Peter and Clarissa have just been reunited, their dwelling on the past is reasonable. It is also convenient for the author, who can thus explore the characters and their past within a fictional context. The emphasis on memory, the past and its effects on the present, and the seeming limits of the future all help to distinguish Clarissa and Septimus. A less ordinary

symbol of time than the clock is the odd, shapeless woman who sings a song with as little apparent sense as it has music (122 - 25). It is an "ancient song," significantly about love and the past. Peter and the Smiths both see her: Peter stops to give her a coin; Lucrezia, her silent sympathy.

11. Exact dates are scattered unobtrusively throughout the work. References to various monarchs and writers offer a sense of time passing as well as approximate dating.

12. Discussions of the relationship between the two women may be found in Bell, II, 115 - 20, 131 - 32, 136 - 40 and in Nicolson, *Portrait of a Marriage*, pp. 200 - 08. Nicolson describes *Orlando* as a "love-letter" (202), Bell says it "commemorates Virginia's love for Vita" (132) and both biographers cite specific parallels between Orlando and Vita. See also Joanna Trautmann, *The Jessamy Brides* (University Park, Penna.: Penn State University Press, 1973).

13. Ironically this is a frequent objection to Quentin Bell's biography of Virginia Woolf. But Bell provides virtually everything a reader could need, including data, careful interpretation of the facts, and (unlike his aunt) documentation of his sources.

14. Supplementing the author's record in her diary, the external history of the writing of *Roger Fry*, including the struggle between author and family, is discussed by Bell; see especially, II, 181 - 83, 207.

15. Letter to Vita Sackville-West, quoted by the recipient in "Virginia Woolf and *Orlando*," *The Listener*, 27 Jan. 1955, p. 157.

Chapter Five

1. See for example pp. 110 - 11: "So that is marriage, Lily thought, a man and a woman looking at a girl throwing a ball. . . . And suddenly the meaning which, for no reason at all . . . descends on people, making them symbolical, making them representative, came upon them, and made them in the dusk standing, looking, the symbols of marriage, husband and wife." Similarly William Bankes finds that a glimpse of Mrs. Ramsay reading James a fairy tale makes him feel that "barbarity was tamed, the reign of chaos subdued" (74). In both instances the individuals briefly become symbolic and thus imbued with immortality.

2. See, for example, F. L. Overcarsh, "The Lighthouse Face to Face," *Accent*, X (Winter 1950), 107 - 23, and Joseph Blotner, "Mythic Patterns in 'To the Lighthouse,'" *PMLA*, LXXI (September 1956), 547 - 62.

3. Other such characters struggling to find order—besides Mr. and Mrs. Ramsay—include Rachel Vinrace and St. John Hirst (*The Voyage Out*), Katharine Hilbery and William Rodney (*Night and Day*), Jacob Flanders (*Jacob's Room*), Orlando (*Orlando*), Bernard, Neville, and Louis (*The Waves*), Peggy Pargiter (*The Years*), and Miss La Trobe (*Between the Acts*).

4. References to water, especially the ocean and its waves, outnumber

by approximately four times the next most prevalent image clusters, those of birds, vegetation, animals, and shapes. Images involving water comprise roughly one-half of those outside the prose-poems.
5. This is one of the many parallels between Bernard and his creator, who observes: "I feel that I am only accumulating notes for a book—whether I shall ever face the labour of writing it, God knows" (AWD, 146).

Chapter Six

1. Leonard Woolf and James Strachey, ed., *Virginia Woolf and Lytton Strachey: Letters* (New York: Harcourt, Brace, 1956), p. 19.
2. There appears to be a discrepancy in dates here: between "midsummer" 1907 and March 1908 is less than a year, but Martin says that Eugénie has been dead "not much more than a year" (148).
3. "Here and Now," besides being a phrase repeatedly used in *The Waves* to refer to the immediate present, appears several times in *A Writer's Diary* as one possible title for *The Years*.
4. See Bell, II, 191 - 96 and *A Writer's Diary*, especially the 1936 entries.
5. Leonard Woolf, *Downhill All The Way*, pp. 145, 155.
6. As Leonard Woolf's Prefatory "Note" explains, the book was all but finished when Virginia Woolf died. It is his belief that the author would have made no substantive changes although many "small corrections" were likely in the final revision.
7. See, for example, AWD, 341. Quentin Bell says that "several drafts for a first chapter remain and two chapters are complete" (II, 222).

Chapter Seven

1. See AWD, 253. She apparently planned this years before choosing the actual format.
2. "The Novels of George Meredith," CE II, 230.

Selected Bibliography

PRIMARY SOURCES

1. Virginia Woolf's   books are published in England by The
   Hogarth Press and in the United States by Harcourt Brace Jovanovich.
   A nearly complete description of the publication history of her
   writings, including various editions of books, first appearances of es-
   says, locations of uncollected reviews, etc., is found in B. J.
   Kirkpatrick's *Bibliography of Virginia Woolf*, 2nd ed. (New York:
   Oxford Univ., 1968). The unpublished diaries and many manuscripts
   are in the Berg Collection of the New York Public Library; additional
   manuscripts are at the British Museum and at the University of Sussex
   Library. Quotations in this study are from the editions listed below:

Between the Acts. New York: Harcourt Brace Jovanovich, 1969.

Books and Portraits. Ed. Mary Lyon. London: Hogarth, 1977.

A Cockney's Farming Experiences. San Diego: San Diego State Univ., 1972
(two stories written at age ten).

Collected Essays, Vol. I. London: Hogarth, 1966; Vol. II - IV. Chatto and
Windus, 1967, 1969. (abbrev. CE)

Contemporary Writers. New York: Harcourt, Brace and World, 1965. (abbrev. CW)

The Diary of Virginia Woolf, Vol. I - V. Ed. Anne Olivier Bell; Introduction
Quentin Bell. Published by Harcourt Brace Jovanovich (New York)
and The Hogarth Press (London), beginning in 1977.

Flush. New York: Harcourt, Brace and World, 1961.

Freshwater: A Comedy. Ed. Lucio P. Ruotolo. New York and London: Harcourt Brace Jovanovich, 1976.

Jacob's Room in *Jacob's Room and The Waves*. New York: Harcourt, Brace
and World, 1950.

A Haunted House and Other Short Stories. New York: Harcourt, Brace and
World, 1972.

The Letters of Virginia Woolf, Vol. I - VI. Ed. Nigel Nicolson and Joanne
Trautmann. Published simultaneously by Harcourt Brace Jovanovich
(New York) and Hogarth Press (London), beginning in 1975.

The London Scene: Five Essays, New York: Frank Hallman, 1975.

*Moments of Being: Unpublished Autobiographical Writings of Virginia
Woolf*. Sussex: The University Press, 1976.

Mrs. Dalloway. New York: Harcourt, Brace and World, 1953.

163

Mrs. Dalloway's Party: A Short Story Sequence. Ed. Stella McNichol. London: Hogarth, 1973.
Night and Day. New York: Harcourt Brace Jovanovich, 1948.
Nurse Lugton's Golden Thimble (a children's story). London: Hogarth, 1966.
Orlando. New York: Harcourt Brace Jovanovich, 1956.
The Pargiters: The Novel - Essay Portion of The Years. Ed. Mitchell A. Leaska. New York: The New York Public Library and Readex Books, 1977.
Roger Fry: A Biography. New York: Harcourt, Brace, 1940.
A Room of One's Own. New York: Harcourt, Brace and World, 1957. (abbrev. *Room*)
Three Guineas. New York: Harcourt, Brace and World, 1966.
To the Lighthouse. New York: Harcourt, Brace and World, 1955.
Virginia Woolf and Lytton Strachey: Letters. Ed. Leonard Woolf and James Strachey. New York: Harcourt, Brace, 1956.
The Voyage Out. New York: Harcourt, Brace and World, 1948.
The Waves in *Jacob's Room and The Waves.* New York: Harcourt, Brace and World, 1959.
A Writer's Diary. Ed. Leonard Woolf. New York: Harcourt Brace Jovanovich, 1954. (abbrev. AWD)
The Years. New York: Harcourt, Brace and World, 1965.

2. Translations (with W. W. Koteliansky):
Dostoevskii, F. M. *Stavrognin's Confession and the Plan of the Life of a Great Sinner.* Richmond, England: L. & V. Woolf, 1922.
Gold'enveizer, A. B. *Talks with Tolstoi.* Richmond, England: L. and V. Woolf, 1923.
Tolstoi, L. H. *Tolstoi's Love Letters with a Study on the Autobiographical Elements in Tolstoi's Work by P. Beryukov.* Richmond, England: L. and V. Woolf, 1923.

SECONDARY SOURCES

   Two issues of *Modern Fiction Studies* devoted to Virginia Woolf include lists of books, chapters, and articles about the author: See the "Checklists" by MAURICE BEEBE, *MFS* (Spring 1956) and BARBARA WISER, *MFS* (Autumn 1972). There are also useful annual reviews in *The Journal of Modern Literature.*
BAZIN, NANCY TOPPING. *Virginia Woolf and the Androgynous Vision.* New Brunswick, N.J.: Rutgers University Press, 1973.
   Relates VW's "vision of reality" and her aesthetics to her psychological condition, and this in turn to her sense of masculine and feminine; thesis - ridden and limited.
BEJA, MORRIS, ed. *Virginia Woolf: To the Lighthouse, A Casebook.* London: MacMillan, 1970.

Collection of extracts, including personal background of author and novel, and nine critical studies: especially useful are three passages on Leslie Stephen.

BELL, QUENTIN. *Virginia Woolf.* New York: Harcourt Brace Jovanovich, 1972.
The standard biography, essential reading.

————. *Bloomsbury.* London: Weidenfeld and Nicolson, 1968. Brief, witty introduction to the Bloomsbury milieu.

BENNETT, JOAN. *Virginia Woolf: Her Art as a Novelist.* New York: Harcourt, Brace, 1945.
Although early, this study of themes and forms is sensitive and broad in scope.

BLACKSTONE, BERNARD. *Virginia Woolf.* New York: Harcourt, Brace, 1949.
What the novels are "about"—freedom, truth, marriage, love, reality; general but useful.

BREWSTER, DOROTHY. *Virginia Woolf.* New York: New York University Press, 1962.
General study with an unusually detailed consideration of VW's essays.

CHAMBERS, R. L. *The Novels of Virginia Woolf.* London: Oliver and Boyd, 1947; rpt. New York: Russell and Russell, 1957.
VW "forged . . . a style and a method" to present the interests she restricted herself to—the internal aspects of human personality; limited but among the better early critiques.

COLLINS, ROBERT G. *Virginia Woolf's Black Arrows of Sensation: The Waves.* Ilfracombe, England: Arthur H. Stockwell, 1962.
Detailed, thoughtful study of themes and characters in a difficult novel make this valuable.

DAICHES, DAVID. *Virginia Woolf.* Norfolk: New Direction, 1942.
Brief appreciative introduction which quotes heavily from the novels and essays as it touches on many themes and techniques; because of its occasional misstatements, this otherwise fine study must be read with special care.

FREEDMAN, RALPH. *The Lyrical Novel: Studies in Herman Hesse, André Gide, and Virginia Woolf.* Princeton, New Jersey: Princeton University Press, 1963.
Considers VW's novels—especially *Mrs. Dalloway, To the Lighthouse,* and *The Waves*—within the specially defined sub - genre of the "lyrical novel"; specialized but excellent.

GADD, DAVID. *The Loving Friends: A Portrait of Bloomsbury.* London: The Hogarth Press, 1974.
An outsider's view of Bloomsbury, focussing on personal relationships; useful for quick overview; interesting reading.

GUIGET, JEAN. *Virginia Woolf and Her Works,* Trans. Jean Stewart. New York: Harcourt, Brace and World, 1965.
Special interests in the creative process and in psychology make this

long and difficult book a valuable study of the relationship between VW's life and her art.

HAFLEY, JAMES. *The Glass Roof: Virginia Woolf as Novelist.* New York: Russell and Russell, 1954; rpt. New York: Russell and Russell, 1963.
The development of VW's ideas and how these affect the forms of the novels; fine, careful study, worth reading.

JOHNSON, MANLY. *Virginia Woolf.* New York: Frederick Ungar, 1973.
Short and superficial general introduction to VW's fiction and feminism.

JOHNSTONE, J. K. *The Bloomsbury Group: A Study of E. M. Forster, Lytton Strachey, Virginia Woolf, and Their Circle.* New York: Noonday, 1954.
The essential text on Bloomsbury; focuses on the philosophical and aesthetic ideas held in common.

KELLY, ALICE VAN BUREN. *The Novels of Virginia Woolf: Fact and Vision.* Chicago: University of Chicago Press, 1973.
Chronological study of the manipulation of a philosophical dichotomy—the relation of fact and vision; its surveys of criticism are more useful than its analyses, though those also have merit.

LATHAM, JACQUELINE E. M., ed. *Critics on Virginia Woolf.* Coral Gables: University of Miami Press, 1970.
Twenty - four extremely short extracts from books and essays; its representativeness makes it a useful introduction to the criticism.

LEASKA, MITCHELL A. *Virginia Woolf's Lighthouse.* New York: Columbia University Press, 1970.
Quantitative study of point-of-view in the novel with some reference to other of VW's works; unusual approach gives this value.

LEHMANN, JOHN. *Virginia Woolf and Her World.* New York: Harcourt Brace Jovanovich, 1976.
Of little use as a biography, this book offers attractive additions to knowledge of VW's social and cultural "world" through its photographs, letters, drawings, etc., and through some anecdotes based on Lehmann's personal associations with Bloomsbury.

LEWIS, THOMAS S. W., ed. *Virginia Woolf.* New York: McGraw - Hill, 1975.
Fourteen critical essays; current, selected bibliography is helpful.

LOVE, JEAN O. *Worlds in Consciousness: Mythopoetic Thought in the Novels of Virginia Woolf.* Berkeley: University of California Press, 1970.
Very theoretical; heavy use of jargon makes the book even less approachable. Second part analyzes novels in terms of the theory described in the first part.

MAJUMDAR, ROBIN and MCLAURIN, ALLEN, ed. *Virginia Woolf: The Critical Heritage.* London: Routledge and Kegan Paul, 1975.
Handy survey of British and American reviews and responses from 1915 to 1941; good introduction.

MARDER, HERBERT. *Feminism and Art.* Chicago: University of Chicago Press, 1968.
Social criticism in the novels and essays; breakdown of the Victorian family, women as a "subject race," androgyny; a reasonable study of a touchy area.

McLAURIN, ALLEN. *Virginia Woolf: The Echoes Enslaved.* Cambridge: Cambridge University Press, 1973.
VW's vision of reality; useful background and textual study.

MOODY, A. D. *Virginia Woolf.* New York: Grove, 1963.
Brief, general; most helpful is the survey of VW's reputation.

NAREMORE, JAMES. *The World Without a Self: Virginia Woolf and the Novel.* New Haven: Yale University Press, 1973.
Good general study of VW's ideas, style, and narrative methods.

NICOLSON, NIGEL. *Portrait of a Marriage: V. Sackville-West and Harold Nicolson.* New York: Atheneum, 1973.
Important background about the relationship between VW and Vita Sackville-West.

NOBLE, JOAN RUSSELL. *Recollections of Virginia Woolf.* New York: William Morrow, 1972.
Anecdotes, reminiscences, and assessments, most written by VW's friends and relatives; interesting supplementary reading.

PIPPETT, AILEEN. *The Moth and the Star: A Biography of Vvirginia Woolf.* Boston: Little, Brown, 1955.
Impressionistic work, superseded by Bell biography. Until full publication of the letters this book remains useful because it contains correspondence between VW and Vita Sackville-West.

RANTAAVARA, IRMA. *Virginia Woolf and Bloomsbury.* Helsinki: Annales Academiae Fennica, 1953.
Supplements Johnstone, Bell, and Gadd.

———. *Virginia Woolf s "The Waves".* Helsinki: Societas scientiarum Fennica, 1960; reprint New York: Kennikat, 1969.
Unusually detailed analysis of a difficult novel gives this study its value; Chapter III ("Language and Style") includes a comprehensive study of VW's vocabulary, syntax, and rhetoric.

RICHTER, HARVENA. *Virginia Woolf: The Inward Voyage.* Princeton, New Jersey: Princeton University Press, 1970.
A psychological study of the "subjective" method of the novels: VW's attempt to find a technique to suit the modern condition and her need to write about herself. Direct, intelligent, and sensible.

ROSENBAUM, S. P., ed. *The Bloomsbury Group.* Toronto: University of Toronto Press, 1975.
Attractive and varied collection of memoirs and comments by and about "members" of the Group.

SCHAEFER, JOSEPHINE O'BRIEN. *The Three-Fold Nature of Reality in the*

Novels of Virginia Woolf. The Hague: Mouton, 1965.
Mediocre general study with a thematic orientation.

SPRAGUE, CLAIRE, ed. *Virginia Woolf: A Collection of Critical Essays.* Englewood Cliffs, New Jersey: Prentice-Hall, 1971.
Introduction plus thirteen standard selections from books and essays; chronology. Good introduction to criticism.

THAKUR, N.C. *The Symbolism of Virginia Woolf.* London: Oxford University Press, 1965.
VW's use of symbols to suggest atmosphere or feeling, to individualize characters, to define types, etc. Solid specialized work.

TRAUTMANN, JOANNE. *The Jessamy Brides: The Friendship of Virginia Woolf and V. Sackville-West.* University Park, Pennsylvania: Pennsylvania State University Press, 1973.
Brief study of the sources and effects of the friendship, including its influence on *Orlando* and on Sackville-West's writings. Less important than Bell or Nicolson.

Virginia Woolf Miscellany. Published by the Department of English, Sonoma State College, California. 1973 -
Edited by various hands, with contributions ranging from book reviews to scholarly notes, information about conferences and manuscripts, anecdotes about VW's life and times or about living in VW's home, this is a delightful and useful newsletter.

Virginia Woolf Quarterly. Vol. I. no 1 (Fall 1972) -
Literary interpretation, analytic essays, primary research, and memoirs related to VW and other members of Bloomsbury; creative writing and visual art sections help make this an attractive repository of current reactions—direct and indirect—to Bloomsbury.

VOGLER, THOMAS A., ed. *Twentieth Century Interpretation of To the Lighthouse.* Englewood Cliffs, New Jersey: Prentice-Hall, 1970.
Introduction plus fourteen essays by thirteen authors; classic selections make this a useful text.

WOODRING, CARL. *Virginia Woolf.* New York: Columbia University Press, 1966.
Introductory study; too brief to be of much use.

WOOLF, LEONARD. *Beginning Again: An Autobiography of the Years 1911 - 1918.* New York: Harcourt, Brace and World, 1964.
_____. *Downhill All the Way: An Autobiography of the Years 1919 - 1939.* London: Hogarth, 1967.
_____. *The Journey Not the Arrival Matters: An Autobiography of the Years 1939 - 1969.* New York: Harcourt, Brace and World. 1969.
These three volumes supplement the biographies and diaries with personal but objective view; chatty, pleasant reading.

Index